EPISTLE TO MARGUERITE DE NAVARRE AND
PREFACE TO A SERMON BY JOHN CALVIN

THE
OTHER VOICE
IN
EARLY MODERN
EUROPE

A Series Edited by Margaret L. King and Albert Rabil Jr.

RECENT BOOKS IN THE SERIES

Marie Dentière

EPISTLE TO MARGUERITE DE NAVARRE AND PREFACE TO A SERMON BY JOHN CALVIN

᠙

Edited and Translated by
Mary B. McKinley

THE UNIVERSITY OF CHICAGO PRESS
Chicago & London

Marie Dentière (1495–1561)

Mary B. McKinley is the Douglas Huntly Gordon Professor of French
at the University of Virginia. She is the author of *Words in a Corner: Studies in
Montaigne's Latin Quotations* and *Les terrains vagues des "Essais": Itinéraires et intertextes.*

The University of Chicago Press, Chicago 60637
The University of Chicago Press, Ltd., London
© 2004 by The University of Chicago
All rights reserved. Published 2004
Printed in the United States of America
13 12 11 10 09 08 07 06 05 04   1 2 3 4 5

ISBN: 0-226-14278-7 (cloth)
ISBN: 0-226-14279-5 (paper)

Library of Congress Cataloging-in-Publication Data

Dentière, Marie, 1495–1561.
  [Epistle to Marguerite de Navarre. English]
  Epistle to Marguerite de Navarre ; and, Preface to a sermon by John Calvin / Marie
Dentière ; edited and translated by Mary B. McKinley.
      p.   cm. — (The other voice in early modern Europe)
  Includes bibliographical references (p.   ) and index.
  ISBN 0-226-14278-7 (cloth : alk. paper) — ISBN 0-226-14279-5 (pbk. : alk. paper)
  1. Reformed Church—Apologetic works.   2. Catholic Church—Controversial
literature.   3. Women's clothing—Biblical teaching.   4. Women—Biblical teaching.
I. Title: Epistle to Marguerite de Navarre ; and, Preface to a sermon by John Calvin.
II. McKinley, Mary B.   III. Dentière, Marie, 1495–1561. Preface to a sermon by John
Calvin. English.   IV. Title: Preface to a sermon by John Calvin.   V. Title.
VI. Series.
BX9422.3.D4613   2004
284'.2—dc22
                                                                              2004005106

♾The paper used in this publication meets the minimum requirements of
the American National Standard for Information Sciences—Permanence
of Paper for Printed Library Materials, ANSI Z39.48-1992.

CONTENTS

ACKNOWLEDGMENTS

I thank Karen Simroth James for acquainting me with Marie Dentière and Jacqueline Cerquiglini Toulet for introducing me to the Musée Historique de la Réformation in Geneva. Cynthia Skenazi shared her work on Dentière with me, and Colette Winn gave me the opportunity to present my early research by hosting the second Femmes Ecrivains sous l'Ancien Régime conference in St. Louis. William Kemp, Diane Desrosiers-Bonin, and Elisabeth Wengler organized the first conference session devoted entirely to Marie Dentière and contributed their important findings in Charlottesville at the fifth conference in that series. Their forthcoming critical edition, prepared in collaboration with other Montreal colleagues, will be a major contribution to our understanding of the Reformation in Geneva and Neuchâtel. I appreciate very much the information they shared with me. Alison Weber and Anne Jacobson Schutte have generously offered valuable advice and support at every stage of this project. Jeffery Persels, George Hoffmann, and Cynthia Skenazi greatly improved the translation and provided key references. Jenny Clay, Ruth Bell, Gregory Hays, and Erik Midelfort helped me to decipher some thorny Latin. Kenny Marotta, Kandioura Drame, Janice Coniglio, Ann Goedde, Amy Ogden, Pascale Barthe, and Cara Welch contributed pertinent observations and speedy assistance. The staff of Alderman Library were quick to help, as usual. Finally, Albert Rabil and Margaret King were encouraging and patient editors, as were Nick Murray and Randy Petilos. I acknowledge with pleasure and gratitude their roles in making this volume possible.

Myra Dickman Orth accompanied me to the Municipal Library in Lunel, helped me to transcribe the preface to Calvin's sermon, answered queries, and offered tips with unfailing generosity and humor. Her death in November 2002 leaves her friends and colleagues bereft. I offer this volume in her memory.

Mary B. McKinley

THE OTHER VOICE IN
EARLY MODERN EUROPE:
INTRODUCTION TO THE SERIES
Margaret L. King and Albert Rabil Jr.

THE OLD VOICE AND THE OTHER VOICE

In western Europe and the United States, women are nearing equality in the professions, in business, and in politics. Most enjoy access to education, reproductive rights, and autonomy in financial affairs. Issues vital to women are on the public agenda: equal pay, child care, domestic abuse, breast cancer research, and curricular revision with an eye to the inclusion of women.

These recent achievements have their origins in things women (and some male supporters) said for the first time about six hundred years ago. Theirs is the "other voice," in contradistinction to the "first voice," the voice of the educated men who created Western culture. Coincident with a general reshaping of European culture in the period 1300–1700 (called the Renaissance or early modern period), questions of female equality and opportunity were raised that still resound and are still unresolved.

The other voice emerged against the backdrop of a three-thousand-year history of the derogation of women rooted in the civilizations related to Western culture: Hebrew, Greek, Roman, and Christian. Negative attitudes toward women inherited from these traditions pervaded the intellectual, medical, legal, religious, and social systems that developed during the European Middle Ages.

The following pages describe the traditional, overwhelmingly male views of women's nature inherited by early modern Europeans and the new tradition that the "other voice" called into being to begin to challenge reigning assumptions. This review should serve as a framework for understanding the texts published in the series the Other Voice in Early Modern Europe. Introductions specific to each text and author follow this essay in all the volumes of the series.

TRADITIONAL VIEWS OF WOMEN, 500 B.C.E.–1500 C.E.

Embedded in the philosophical and medical theories of the ancient Greeks were perceptions of the female as inferior to the male in both mind and body. Similarly, the structure of civil legislation inherited from the ancient Romans was biased against women, and the views on women developed by Christian thinkers out of the Hebrew Bible and the Christian New Testament were negative and disabling. Literary works composed in the vernacular of ordinary people, and widely recited or read, conveyed these negative assumptions. The social networks within which most women lived—those of the family and the institutions of the Roman Catholic Church—were shaped by this negative tradition and sharply limited the areas in which women might act in and upon the world.

GREEK PHILOSOPHY AND FEMALE NATURE. Greek biology assumed that women were inferior to men and defined them as merely childbearers and housekeepers. This view was authoritatively expressed in the works of the philosopher Aristotle.

Aristotle thought in dualities. He considered action superior to inaction, form (the inner design or structure of any object) superior to matter, completion to incompletion, possession to deprivation. In each of these dualities, he associated the male principle with the superior quality and the female with the inferior. "The male principle in nature," he argued, "is associated with active, formative and perfected characteristics, while the female is passive, material and deprived, desiring the male in order to become complete."[1] Men are always identified with virile qualities, such as judgment, courage, and stamina, and women with their opposites—irrationality, cowardice, and weakness.

The masculine principle was considered superior even in the womb. The man's semen, Aristotle believed, created the form of a new human creature, while the female body contributed only matter. (The existence of the ovum, and with it the other facts of human embryology, was not established until the seventeenth century.) Although the later Greek physician Galen believed there was a female component in generation, contributed by "female semen," the followers of both Aristotle and Galen saw the male role in human generation as more active and more important.

In the Aristotelian view, the male principle sought always to reproduce itself. The creation of a female was always a mistake, therefore, resulting

---

1. Aristotle, *Physics* 1.9.192a20–24, in *The Complete Works of Aristotle*, ed. Jonathan Barnes, rev. Oxford trans., 2 vols. (Princeton, 1984), 1:328.

from an imperfect act of generation. Every female born was considered a "defective" or "mutilated" male (as Aristotle's terminology has variously been translated), a "monstrosity" of nature.[2]

For Greek theorists, the biology of males and females was the key to their psychology. The female was softer and more docile, more apt to be despondent, querulous, and deceitful. Being incomplete, moreover, she craved sexual fulfillment in intercourse with a male. The male was intellectual, active, and in control of his passions.

These psychological polarities derived from the theory that the universe consisted of four elements (earth, fire, air, and water), expressed in human bodies as four "humors" (black bile, yellow bile, blood, and phlegm) considered, respectively, dry, hot, damp, and cold and corresponding to mental states ("melancholic," "choleric," "sanguine," "phlegmatic"). In this scheme the male, sharing the principles of earth and fire, was dry and hot; the female, sharing the principles of air and water, was cold and damp.

Female psychology was further affected by her dominant organ, the uterus (womb), *hystera* in Greek. The passions generated by the womb made women lustful, deceitful, talkative, irrational, indeed—when these affects were in excess—"hysterical."

Aristotle's biology also had social and political consequences. If the male principle was superior and the female inferior, then in the household, as in the state, men should rule and women must be subordinate. That hierarchy did not rule out the companionship of husband and wife, whose cooperation was necessary for the welfare of children and the preservation of property. Such mutuality supported male preeminence.

Aristotle's teacher Plato suggested a different possibility: that men and women might possess the same virtues. The setting for this proposal is the imaginary and ideal Republic that Plato sketches in a dialogue of that name. Here, for a privileged elite capable of leading wisely, all distinctions of class and wealth dissolve, as, consequently, do those of gender. Without households or property, as Plato constructs his ideal society, there is no need for the subordination of women. Women may therefore be educated to the same level as men to assume leadership. Plato's Republic remained imaginary, however. In real societies, the subordination of women remained the norm and the prescription.

The views of women inherited from the Greek philosophical tradition became the basis for medieval thought. In the thirteenth century, the supreme Scholastic philosopher Thomas Aquinas, among others, still echoed

2. Aristotle, *Generation of Animals* 2.3.737a27–28, in *The Complete Works*, 1:1144.

Aristotle's views of human reproduction, of male and female personalities, and of the preeminent male role in the social hierarchy.

ROMAN LAW AND THE FEMALE CONDITION. Roman law, like Greek philosophy, underlay medieval thought and shaped medieval society. The ancient belief that adult property-owning men should administer households and make decisions affecting the community at large is the very fulcrum of Roman law.

About 450 B.C.E., during Rome's republican era, the community's customary law was recorded (legendarily) on twelve tablets erected in the city's central forum. It was later elaborated by professional jurists whose activity increased in the imperial era, when much new legislation was passed, especially on issues affecting family and inheritance. This growing, changing body of laws was eventually codified in the *Corpus of Civil Law* under the direction of the emperor Justinian, generations after the empire ceased to be ruled from Rome. That *Corpus*, read and commented on by medieval scholars from the eleventh century on, inspired the legal systems of most of the cities and kingdoms of Europe.

Laws regarding dowries, divorce, and inheritance pertain primarily to women. Since those laws aimed to maintain and preserve property, the women concerned were those from the property-owning minority. Their subordination to male family members points to the even greater subordination of lower-class and slave women, about whom the laws speak little.

In the early republic, the *paterfamilias*, or "father of the family," possessed *patria potestas*, "paternal power." The term *pater*, "father," in both these cases does not necessarily mean biological father but denotes the head of a household. The father was the person who owned the household's property and, indeed, its human members. The *paterfamilias* had absolute power—including the power, rarely exercised, of life or death—over his wife, his children, and his slaves, as much as his cattle.

Male children could be "emancipated," an act that granted legal autonomy and the right to own property. Those over fourteen could be emancipated by a special grant from the father or automatically by their father's death. But females could never be emancipated; instead, they passed from the authority of their father to that of a husband or, if widowed or orphaned while still unmarried, to a guardian or tutor.

Marriage in its traditional form placed the woman under her husband's authority, or *manus*. He could divorce her on grounds of adultery, drinking wine, or stealing from the household, but she could not divorce him. She could neither possess property in her own right nor bequeath any to her children upon her death. When her husband died, the household property passed not to her but to his male heirs. And when her father died, she had no claim to any family inheritance, which was directed to her brothers or more remote male relatives. The effect of these laws was to exclude women from civil society, itself based on property ownership.

In the later republican and imperial periods, these rules were significantly modified. Women rarely married according to the traditional form. The practice of "free" marriage allowed a woman to remain under her father's authority, to possess property given her by her father (most frequently the "dowry," recoverable from the husband's household on his death), and to inherit from her father. She could also bequeath property to her own children and divorce her husband, just as he could divorce her.

Despite this greater freedom, women still suffered enormous disability under Roman law. Heirs could belong only to the father's side, never the mother's. Moreover, although she could bequeath her property to her children, she could not establish a line of succession in doing so. A woman was "the beginning and end of her own family," said the jurist Ulpian. Moreover, women could play no public role. They could not hold public office, represent anyone in a legal case, or even witness a will. Women had only a private existence and no public personality.

The dowry system, the guardian, women's limited ability to transmit wealth, and total political disability are all features of Roman law adopted by the medieval communities of western Europe, although modified according to local customary laws.

CHRISTIAN DOCTRINE AND WOMEN'S PLACE. The Hebrew Bible and the Christian New Testament authorized later writers to limit women to the realm of the family and to burden them with the guilt of original sin. The passages most fruitful for this purpose were the creation narratives in Genesis and sentences from the Epistles defining women's role within the Christian family and community.

Each of the first two chapters of Genesis contains a creation narrative. In the first "God created man in his own image, in the image of God he created him; male and female he created them" (Gn 1:27). In the second, God created Eve from Adam's rib (2:21–23). Christian theologians relied principally on Genesis 2 for their understanding of the relation between man and woman, interpreting the creation of Eve from Adam as proof of her subordination to him.

The creation story in Genesis 2 leads to that of the temptations in Genesis 3: of Eve by the wily serpent and of Adam by Eve. As read by Christian theologians from Tertullian to Thomas Aquinas, the narrative made Eve responsible for the Fall and its consequences. She instigated the act; she deceived her husband; she suffered the greater punishment. Her disobedience made it necessary for Jesus to be incarnated and to die on the cross. From the pulpit, moralists and preachers for centuries conveyed to women the guilt that they bore for original sin.

The Epistles offered advice to early Christians on building communities of the faithful. Among the matters to be regulated was the place of women. Paul offered views favorable to women in Galatians 3:28: "There is neither Jew nor Greek, there is neither slave nor free, there is neither male nor female; for you are all one in Christ Jesus." Paul also referred to women as his coworkers and placed them on a par with himself and his male coworkers (Phlm 4:2–3; Rom 16:1–3; 1 Cor 16:19). Elsewhere, Paul limited women's possibilities: "But I want you to understand that the head of every man is Christ, the head of a woman is her husband, and the head of Christ is God" (1 Cor 11:3).

Biblical passages by later writers (although attributed to Paul) enjoined women to forgo jewels, expensive clothes, and elaborate coiffures; and they forbade women to "teach or have authority over men," telling them to "learn in silence with all submissiveness" as is proper for one responsible for sin, consoling them, however, with the thought that they will be saved through childbearing (1 Tm 2:9–15). Other texts among the later Epistles defined women as the weaker sex and emphasized their subordination to their husbands (1 Pt 3:7; Col 3:18; Eph 5:22–23).

These passages from the New Testament became the arsenal employed by theologians of the early church to transmit negative attitudes toward women to medieval Christian culture—above all, Tertullian (*On the Apparel of Women*), Jerome (*Against Jovinian*), and Augustine (*The Literal Meaning of Genesis*).

THE IMAGE OF WOMEN IN MEDIEVAL LITERATURE. The philosophical, legal, and religious traditions born in antiquity formed the basis of the medieval intellectual synthesis wrought by trained thinkers, mostly clerics, writing in Latin and based largely in universities. The vernacular literary tradition that developed alongside the learned tradition also spoke about female nature and women's roles. Medieval stories, poems, and epics also portrayed women negatively—as lustful and deceitful—while praising good housekeepers and loyal wives as replicas of the Virgin Mary or the female saints and martyrs.

There is an exception in the movement of "courtly love" that evolved in southern France from the twelfth century. Courtly love was the erotic love between a nobleman and noblewoman, the latter usually superior in social

women, in Latin and in the vernaculars: works enumerating the achievements of notable women; works rebutting the main accusations made against women; works arguing for the equal education of men and women; works defining and redefining women's proper role in the family, at court, in public; works describing women's lives and experiences. Recent monographs and articles have begun to hint at the great range of this movement, involving probably several thousand titles. The protofeminism of these "other voices" constitutes a significant fraction of the literary product of the early modern era.

THE CATALOGS. About 1365, the same Boccaccio whose *Corbaccio* rehearses the usual charges against female nature wrote another work, *Concerning Famous Women*. A humanist treatise drawing on classical texts, it praised 106 notable women: ninety-eight of them from pagan Greek and Roman antiquity, one (Eve) from the Bible, and seven from the medieval religious and cultural tradition; his book helped make all readers aware of a sex normally condemned or forgotten. Boccaccio's outlook nevertheless was unfriendly to women, for it singled out for praise those women who possessed the traditional virtues of chastity, silence, and obedience. Women who were active in the public realm—for example, rulers and warriors—were depicted as usually being lascivious and as suffering terrible punishments for entering the masculine sphere. Women were his subject, but Boccaccio's standard remained male.

Christine de Pizan's *Book of the City of Ladies* contains a second catalog, one responding specifically to Boccaccio's. Whereas Boccaccio portrays female virtue as exceptional, she depicts it as universal. Many women in history were leaders, or remained chaste despite the lascivious approaches of men, or were visionaries and brave martyrs.

The work of Boccaccio inspired a series of catalogs of illustrious women of the biblical, classical, Christian, and local pasts, among them Filippo da Bergamo's *Of Illustrious Women*, Pierre de Brantôme's *Lives of Illustrious Women*, Pierre Le Moyne's *Gallerie of Heroic Women*, and Pietro Paolo de Ribera's *Immortal Triumphs and Heroic Enterprises of 845 Women*. Whatever their embedded prejudices, these works drove home to the public the possibility of female excellence.

THE DEBATE. At the same time, many questions remained: Could a woman be virtuous? Could she perform noteworthy deeds? Was she even, strictly speaking, of the same human species as men? These questions were debated over four centuries, in French, German, Italian, Spanish, and English, by authors male and female, among Catholics, Protestants, and Jews, in ponderous volumes and breezy pamphlets. The whole literary genre has been called the *querelle des femmes*, the "woman question."

The opening volley of this battle occurred in the first years of the fifteenth century, in a literary debate sparked by Christine de Pizan. She exchanged letters critical of Jean de Meun's contribution to *The Romance of the Rose* with two French royal secretaries, Jean de Montreuil and Gontier Col. When the matter became public, Jean Gerson, one of Europe's leading theologians, supported de Pizan's arguments against de Meun, for the moment silencing the opposition.

The debate resurfaced repeatedly over the next two hundred years. *The Triumph of Women* (1438) by Juan Rodríguez de la Camara (or Juan Rodríguez del Padron) struck a new note by presenting arguments for the superiority of women to men. *The Champion of Women* (1440–42) by Martin Le Franc addresses once again the negative views of women presented in *The Romance of the Rose* and offers counterevidence of female virtue and achievement.

A cameo of the debate on women is included in *The Courtier*, one of the most widely read books of the era, published by the Italian Baldassare Castiglione in 1528 and immediately translated into other European vernaculars. *The Courtier* depicts a series of evenings at the court of the duke of Urbino in which many men and some women of the highest social stratum amuse themselves by discussing a range of literary and social issues. The "woman question" is a pervasive theme throughout, and the third of its four books is devoted entirely to that issue.

In a verbal duel, Gasparo Pallavicino and Giuliano de' Medici present the main claims of the two traditions. Gasparo argues the innate inferiority of women and their inclination to vice. Only in bearing children do they profit the world. Giuliano counters that women share the same spiritual and mental capacities as men and may excel in wisdom and action. Men and women are of the same essence: just as no stone can be more perfectly a stone than another, so no human being can be more perfectly human than others, whether male or female. It was an astonishing assertion, boldly made to an audience as large as all Europe.

THE TREATISES. Humanism provided the materials for a positive counterconcept to the misogyny embedded in Scholastic philosophy and law and inherited from the Greek, Roman, and Christian pasts. A series of humanist treatises on marriage and family, on education and deportment, and on the nature of women helped construct these new perspectives.

The works by Francesco Barbaro and Leon Battista Alberti—*On Marriage*

(1415) and *On the Family* (1434–37)—far from defending female equality, reasserted women's responsibility for rearing children and managing the housekeeping while being obedient, chaste, and silent. Nevertheless, they served the cause of reexamining the issue of women's nature by placing domestic issues at the center of scholarly concern and reopening the pertinent classical texts. In addition, Barbaro emphasized the companionate nature of marriage and the importance of a wife's spiritual and mental qualities for the well-being of the family.

These themes reappear in later humanist works on marriage and the education of women by Juan Luis Vives and Erasmus. Both were moderately sympathetic to the condition of women without reaching beyond the usual masculine prescriptions for female behavior.

An outlook more favorable to women characterizes the nearly unknown work *In Praise of Women* (ca. 1487) by the Italian humanist Bartolommeo Goggio. In addition to providing a catalog of illustrious women, Goggio argued that male and female are the same in essence, but that women (reworking the Adam and Eve narrative from quite a new angle) are actually superior. In the same vein, the Italian humanist Mario Equicola asserted the spiritual equality of men and women in *On Women* (1501). In 1525, Galeazzo Flavio Capra (or Capella) published his work *On the Excellence and Dignity of Women*. This humanist tradition of treatises defending the worthiness of women culminates in the work of Henricus Cornelius Agrippa *On the Nobility and Preeminence of the Female Sex*. No work by a male humanist more succinctly or explicitly presents the case for female dignity.

THE WITCH BOOKS. While humanists grappled with the issues pertaining to women and family, other learned men turned their attention to what they perceived as a very great problem: witches. Witch-hunting manuals, explorations of the witch phenomenon, and even defenses of witches are not at first glance pertinent to the tradition of the other voice. But they do relate in this way: most accused witches were women. The hostility aroused by supposed witch activity is comparable to the hostility aroused by women. The evil deeds the victims of the hunt were charged with were exaggerations of the vices to which, many believed, all women were prone.

The connection between the witch accusation and the hatred of women is explicit in the notorious witch-hunting manual *The Hammer of Witches* (1486) by two Dominican inquisitors, Heinrich Krämer and Jacob Sprenger. Here the inconstancy, deceitfulness, and lustfulness traditionally associated with women are depicted in exaggerated form as the core features of witch behavior. These traits inclined women to make a bargain with the devil—sealed by sexual intercourse—by which they acquired unholy powers. Such bizarre claims, far from being rejected by rational men, were broadcast by intellectuals. The German Ulrich Molitur, the Frenchman Nicolas Rémy, and the Italian Stefano Guazzo all coolly informed the public of sinister orgies and midnight pacts with the devil. The celebrated French jurist, historian, and political philosopher Jean Bodin argued that because women were especially prone to diabolism, regular legal procedures could properly be suspended in order to try those accused of this "exceptional crime."

A few experts such as the physician Johann Weyer, a student of Agrippa's, raised their voices in protest. In 1563, he explained the witch phenomenon thus, without discarding belief in diabolism: the devil deluded foolish old women afflicted by melancholia, causing them to believe they had magical powers. Weyer's rational skepticism, which had good credibility in the community of the learned, worked to revise the conventional views of women and witchcraft.

WOMEN'S WORKS. To the many categories of works produced on the question of women's worth must be added nearly all works written by women. A woman writing was in herself a statement of women's claim to dignity.

Only a few women wrote anything before the dawn of the modern era, for three reasons. First, they rarely received the education that would enable them to write. Second, they were not admitted to the public roles—as administrator, bureaucrat, lawyer or notary, or university professor—in which they might gain knowledge of the kinds of things the literate public thought worth writing about. Third, the culture imposed silence on women, considering speaking out a form of unchastity. Given these conditions, it is remarkable that any women wrote. Those who did before the fourteenth century were almost always nuns or religious women whose isolation made their pronouncements more acceptable.

From the fourteenth century on, the volume of women's writings rose. Women continued to write devotional literature, although not always as cloistered nuns. They also wrote diaries, often intended as keepsakes for their children; books of advice to their sons and daughters; letters to family members and friends; and family memoirs, in a few cases elaborate enough to be considered histories.

A few women wrote works directly concerning the "woman question," and some of these, such as the humanists Isotta Nogarola, Cassandra Fedele, Laura Cereta, and Olympia Morata, were highly trained. A few were professional writers, living by the income of their pens; the very first among them

educated to the same standard as male leaders would they be able to raise that other voice and insist on their dignity as human beings morally, intellectually, and legally equal to men.

THE OTHER VOICE. The other voice, a voice of protest, was mostly female, but it was also male. It spoke in the vernaculars and in Latin, in treatises and dialogues, in plays and poetry, in letters and diaries, and in pamphlets. It battered at the wall of prejudice that encircled women and raised a banner announcing its claims. The female was equal (or even superior) to the male in essential nature—moral, spiritual, and intellectual. Women were capable of higher education, of holding positions of power and influence in the public realm, and of speaking and writing persuasively. The last bastion of masculine supremacy, centered on the notions of a woman's primary domestic responsibility and the requirement of female chastity, was not as yet assaulted—although visions of productive female communities as alternatives to the family indicated an awareness of the problem.

During the period 1300–1700, the other voice remained only a voice, and one only dimly heard. It did not result—yet—in an alteration of social patterns. Indeed, to this day they have not entirely been altered. Yet the call for justice issued as long as six centuries ago by those writing in the tradition of the other voice must be recognized as the source and origin of the mature feminist tradition and of the realignment of social institutions accomplished in the modern age.

We thank the volume editors in this series, who responded with many suggestions to an earlier draft of this introduction, making it a collaborative enterprise. Many of their suggestions and criticisms have resulted in revisions of this introduction, although we remain responsible for the final product.

PROJECTED TITLES IN THE SERIES

Isabella Andreini, *Mirtilla*, edited and translated by Laura Stortoni

Tullia d'Aragona, *Complete Poems and Letters*, edited and translated by Julia Hairston

Tullia d'Aragona, *The Wretch, Otherwise Known as Guerrino*, edited and translated by Julia Hairston and John McLucas

Giuseppa Eleonora Barbapiccola and Diamante Medaglia Faini, *The Education of Women*, edited and translated by Rebecca Messbarger

Francesco Barbaro et al., *On Marriage and the Family*, edited and translated by Margaret L. King

Laura Battiferra, *Selected Poetry, Prose, and Letters*, edited and translated by Victoria Kirkham

VOLUME EDITOR'S
INTRODUCTION

THE OTHER VOICE

Marie Dentière walks onto the stage of Reformation Geneva in fleeting, intermittent scenes. Her appearances, although brief, are always dramatic. Her voice emerges in several sixteenth-century documents related to the Reformed Church takeover in Geneva and John Calvin's subsequent dominance there. It speaks with authority and passion about crucial issues in the struggle between the reformers and the Catholic Church, and it claims a vital role for women as teachers of religious doctrine and morals. An early supporter of the French reform movement and later of Guillaume Farel and Calvin in their mission to the French-speaking Swiss, Dentière knew both good times and bad in her relations with her fellow reformers. She accompanied Farel as an active partner in at least one proselytizing effort, and she protested vigorously when Farel and Calvin were expelled from Geneva.

The glimpses we get of Dentière through contemporary documents are nevertheless colored by scorn, an attitude that persisted in one prominent nineteenth-century editor's comments about her. However, the works that bear her name—or, more precisely in some cases, her initials—reveal a learned mind well-versed in the Bible and conversant with Catholic Church doctrine as well as the theological and polemical writings of Farel, Calvin and their circles.[1] From the 1520s until 1561, the year of her death, this outspoken woman remained seemingly undaunted in the face of censure, sup-

---

1. Excellent introductions to many of the people, places, and issues mentioned here appear in *The Oxford Encyclopedia of the Reformation*, ed. Hillerbrand; *The Oxford Dictionary of the Christian Church*, ed. Cross; *Contemporaries of Erasmus*, ed. Bietenholz and Deutscher; and *A Catholic Dictionary of Theology*. Francis Higman provides useful precision of terminology in his *La diffusion de la Réforme en France, 1520–1565* (4–5). The word *protestant*, for example, emerged to describe those who protested against the decisions of the 1529 Diet of Speyer; it originally designated only followers of Luther and only later came to be a generic term for all those who rejected the Catholic Church.

pression, and ridicule. Her *Very Useful Epistle* (1539) is the first explicit statement of reformed theology by a woman to appear in French. Addressed to
Marguerite de Navarre, sister of the French King Francis I and early supporter of the reform movement in France, it shows two women from very different backgrounds, each of whom dared to defy authority and convention
by expressing in print their dissident religious convictions. Dentière's preface
to one of Calvin's sermons, published in 1561, shows that she remained actively involved in religious reform to the end of her life.

LIFE AND CAREER

After a century of almost total neglect, Marie Dentière—or d'Ennetières—
has recently become the object of renewed scholarly inquiry. The available
biographical information about her leaves many questions unanswered.[2]
Born in 1495 to a noble family in Tournai, she entered an Augustinian convent in that city. Martin Luther's ideas had attracted strong interest and support in Tournai and the nearby areas of northern France and the Low
Countries, and the Augustinians, Luther's order, were particularly open to religious reform.[3] In the early 1520s, Dentière left the convent and eventually
arrived in Strasbourg. She married Simon Robert, a former priest from Tournai who joined the French reformers in Strasbourg in 1525. Her early life
thus follows a familiar trajectory for women involved in the Reformation.
That movement generally rejected the Catholic rule of celibacy for its clergy
and placed greater spiritual value on marriage. It also offered hope for a better education for women and a more active role for women in the church, a
hope that was not always fulfilled.[4]

2. The spelling of her family name is irregular in sixteenth-century documents. Dentière is the
spelling that appears on the Mazarine copy of the *Epistle* and in Jeanne de Jussie's *Petit chronique*.
D'Ennetières is the form of her family name in Tournai preferred by Kemp and Desrosiers-Bonin
(see below) and Moreau (see n. 3). A good introduction to her life and work is Head, "A Propagandist for the Reform:." Still valuable is the Henri Bordier's article on Marie Dentière in Haag,
ed., *La France protestante*, 238–49. See also Dufour, *Notice bibliographique sur le Cathéchisme et la Confession de foi de Calvin*, 155–59; Berthoud, *Antoine Marcourt, réformateur et pamphlétaire*, 65–70; Head,
"The Religion of the *Femmelettes*"; Backus, "Marie Dentière"; Thompson, *John Calvin and the Daughters of Sarah*, 40–45; Bothe, "Ecriture féminine de la Réformation: le témoignage de Marie Dentière"; and Skenazi, "Marie Dentière et la prédication des femmes." William Kemp and Diane
Desrosiers-Bonin have recently contributed important new information in "Marie d'Ennetières
et la petite grammaire hébraïque."

3. Moreau, *Histoire du Protestantisme à Tournai*, 63–64.

4. The articles on "Marriage" and "Defenses of Marriage" in Hillerbrand, ed., *The Oxford Encyclopedia of the Reformation* give a good overview of the reformers' positions on women and marriage.
For the promise that religious reform offered women, see Roelker, "The Appeal of Calvinism to

Information about Marie Dentière's sojourn in Strasbourg is sketchy at best. Here, as in general throughout her life, she is identified not by her own name but by her relationship to her husband: she is *uxor Symonis*, Simon's wife.[5] Much of what we can know about her must be gleaned from those references. However, she entered Strasbourg society at a moment when the city offered unprecedented opportunities for contact among major figures in the Reform movement, as well as new models for active involvement of women in the church. During those years Strasbourg was rapidly becoming an important center of Reformation activity and a site of dialogue between French and German advocates for religious change.[6] Martin Bucer, a former Dominican, arrived there in 1523 and faced harsh criticism for having renounced his monastic vows and married a "prostituted woman," a former cloistered nun. Bucer became both a leader of the Reformation and a major actor in ecumenical efforts to mediate between Lutherans and Zwinglians and to seek reconciliation with Catholics. He would later welcome John Calvin to Strasbourg when Calvin was expelled from Geneva in 1538. By that date, Strasbourg had long since established its reputation as a refuge for the French reformers known as "evangelical" from the French word for Gospel, *évangile*.

In 1525, with King Francis held captive in Madrid after his military defeat at Pavia, the Parisian Parlement, encouraged by the Faculty of Theology, known by its critics as the Sorbonne, moved to arrest and prosecute leaders of the evangelical reform movement in the diocese of Meaux. In her brother's absence, Marguerite, Duchess of Alençon, later Queen of Navarre, was hampered in her efforts to protect the Meaux group, whose bishop, Guillaume Briçonnet, was her spiritual director.[7] Lefèvre d'Etaples, the aging father of the evangelical reform, along with Gérard Roussel and Michel Arande, personal chaplains of Marguerite, sought refuge in Strasbourg in autumn, 1525. Guillaume Farel, a zealous French advocate of evangelical reform from the Dauphiné and a former student of Lefèvre's in Paris, had arrived there in April

---

French Noblewomen in the Sixteenth Century"; Davis, *Society and Culture in Early Modern France* (see the chapter "City Women and Religious Change," 65–95). Opinions differ about whether or not the Reformation improved the situation of women. See Head, "Religion of the *Femmelettes*"; and Douglass, "Women and the Continental Reformation."

5. Herminjard, *Correspondance des Réformateurs*; see, for example, 2: 127 (no. 230). I refer to Herminjard by volume and page number, followed by letter number in parenthesis.

6. See Chrisman, *Strasbourg and the Reform*.

7. See Heller, "Marguerite de Navarre and the Reformers of Meaux"; and Farge, "Marguerite de Navarre, Her Circle, and the Censors of Paris." Jonathan Reid's doctoral dissertation, "King's Sister, Queen of Dissent," gives the most complete account of the movement and the queen's involvement in it.

of that year. He was to become the most important figure in reforming the churches of French-speaking Switzerland.[8] The French were welcomed as guests of Wolfgang Capito, a former Catholic theologian and Hebrew scholar who embraced the reform movement shortly after arriving in Strasbourg in 1523. Capito's home became a meeting place for the French scholars, a safe haven where Lefèvre and Roussel worked on the translation of the Bible from Hebrew and Greek into French. Hebrew scholarship later became an activity in Marie Dentière's own household.

The Strasbourg reformers' community included educated, articulate women.[9] Following Martin Bucer, several other Catholic priests married and wrote strong defenses of clerical marriage. In December 1523, Matthias Zell, a priest and popular preacher in the cathedral parish, married Katharina Schütz, the young daughter of a prominent Strasbourg family who had embraced evangelical reform after reading Martin Luther's works. When Matthias Zell was attacked for having corrupted her, Katharina Zell responded in 1524 by writing a defense of her husband and of clerical marriage.[10] Katharina Zell became an active partner in her husband's ministry and wrote and published in her own name. She addressed a pamphlet of consolation to the wives of men obliged to seek refuge in Strasbourg because of their religious convictions, and she published an edition in German of a Bohemian hymn book with a preface instructing lay people on devotional reform. She corresponded with Luther and other reformed ministers. When Matthias Zell died in 1548, Katharina defied the convention against women conducting religious services by delivering a sermon at her husband's funeral.[11] Like Capito and other Strasbourg reform leaders, the Zell family opened their home to foreign reformed converts seeking refuge in the city. In that hospitable community in the mid-1520s, Marie Dentière would have seen in Katharina Zell a woman who was a partner in her husband's pastoral work and a published theologian and advocate of the reformed religion in her own right.

In 1528 Simon Robert and Marie Dentière left Strasbourg to follow

8. The most detailed account of Farel's life and work and of the Neuchâtel reform is *Guillaume Farel, 1489–1565: Biographie nouvelle*. Much of Farel's correspondence, as well as other important letters pertaining to the Reformation of French-speaking countries and to Marie Dentière and her husbands, is recorded in Herminjard, *Correspondance des Réformateurs*.

9. See Chrisman, "Women and the Reformation in Strasbourg, 1490–1530"; and McKee, *Katharina Schütz Zell*, 1: 29–49 (ch. 2, "The Coming of the Protestant Reformation and the Birth of a Partnership").

10. Katharina Zell's defense will be published in this series.

11. See McKee's biography, vol. 1 of *Katharina Schütz Zell*.

Guillaume Farel in his mission to establish the reformed religion in the Valais, the Rhône valley region east of Lake Geneva. They were the first French married couple to accept a pastoral assignment for the Reformed Church. Martin Bucer, writing to Farel, who was already in the Valais, alerted him about the couple's arrival, referring to "Simon's wife" as an active party in their ministry.[12] Against the protests of the local clergy, including the established vicar, Simon Robert became pastor of the church at Bex.[13] Soon thereafter he moved with his wife to assume the same position at nearby Aigle, where they were in close contact with neighboring pastors Farel and his young follower, Antoine Froment, a compatriot of Farel from the Dauphiné. In 1533 Robert died, leaving his widow with several young children. Marie Dentière married Antoine Froment as he was becoming prominently involved in the events leading to the reformers' takeover of Geneva. The couple settled in the city in 1535.

THE REFORMATION IN GENEVA

In the decades preceding 1536, the year the reformers succeeded in expelling the Catholic clergy from the city, Geneva had undergone political upheaval and a major transformation of its governing bodies. Those changes prepared the way for religious reform. Geneva had long been an episcopal city-state ruled by a prince-bishop and largely controlled by the duke of Savoy, who ruled an area in what is now Alpine France and the Italian Piedmont. Catholic clergy exercised power over ecclesiastical matters, but they also often manipulated temporal affairs and civil government. The municipal government consisted of an elected General Council led by magistrates called syndics. In the 1520s gradual rebellion against the Savoyard rule had begun to challenge the sovereignty of the bishop and his ecclesiastical officers. The syndics and the council began to negotiate directly with city-states of the Swiss confederacy, notably with Berne and Fribourg, centers of power that were independent and often hostile to the dukes of Savoy. In 1527 the bishop of Geneva conceded to the newly instituted Council of Two Hundred the right to control civil and judicial proceedings.[14]

As those political events were unfolding, and facilitated by them, religious reform moved into Geneva. In autumn 1532 Guillaume Farel arrived in

12. Herminjard, *Correspondance*, 2: 126 (no. 230).

13. Ibid., 2: 141 (no. 238).

14. On these events, see Kingdon, "Was the Protestant Reformation a Revolution?"; Ozment, "Calvin and Calvinism"; and Naef, *Les origines de la Réforme à Genève*.

the city and established a reputation as a charismatic preacher. Farel was soon evicted, but he would return often to Geneva along with fellow missioners Froment and Pierre Viret, attracting other converts to the reformed religion. Pamphlets and placards attacking the Catholic church began to circulate. By the end of the year, French immigrants had established an evangelical community in the city. On January 1, 1533, Antoine Froment preached the first public reformed sermon to a large gathering on the Molard, a central public square.[15] In January 1534, Farel and Viret opposed Guy Furbity, a Dominican friar supporting the Roman Catholic position, in a public debate on religion that ended in a riot. Civic unrest grew, and violent incidents became more frequent. Savoyard militia ravaged the countryside around Geneva, disrupting commerce and threatening the city's food supply. In 1535, the Genevan city magistrates suspended the celebration of mass in all city churches, giving Catholic clergy the option of converting to the new evangelical reform or leaving the city. In May 1536, a general assembly of Geneva's citizens declared its allegiance to the Reformation and pledged to abolish "papal abuses." The reformed religion had won the city. Calvin arrived there for the first time two months later for what he intended to be a brief visit, and Farel persuaded him to stay and help him organize the new Reformed Church.

The earliest work that has been attributed to Marie Dentière is a history of the reformers' victory in Geneva, *La guerre et délivrance de la ville de Genesve fidèlement faicte et composée par un Marchand demourant en icelle* [The war and deliverance of the city of Geneva, faithfully told and written by a merchant living in that city], originally published in 1536.[16] That book recounts the events of 1532–36 from the point of view of the reformers. From the first page, it attributes their victory purely to divine intervention. "One must not be astonished that God so miraculously delivered us from our enemies asking nothing in return, without our having merited or deserved it, because God always shows his virtue and strength in cases where men have despaired" (35). Nevertheless, the story chronicles the heroism of men. It portrays the events leading to victory as a struggle between powerful evil forces and the valiant

---

15. Froment reproduced the sermon as he remembered it in his later chronicle of those years in Geneva, *Les actes et gestes merveilleux de la cité de Genève*, 22–29. See under "Fromment" in the bibliography; the spelling of his name varies, and his editor used Anthoine Fromment, though the more common spelling is Antoine Froment.

16. See *La guerre et deslivrance de la ville de Genesve*. There is no known surviving copy of the 1536 edition of *The War and Deliverance*. The publisher, Albert Rilliet, worked from a manuscript copy of the printed edition, correcting an earlier 1863 edition that accepted the merchant as author and that was made from yet another manuscript, one that Rilliet argued was faulty. Page numbers are cited parenthetically in the text. The work is entered by title in the bibliography because I think the attribution to Marie Dentière is unlikely.

few who had faith in God's power. It presents the Catholic duke, bishops, and priests as tyrants who did not hesitate to seize the goods of the Genevan citizens, "even the lives, the wives and daughters of the good merchants, who were not safe with their parents and relatives, but were raped and abducted by force from their own husbands" (40). Calling on examples from the Old Testament, it portrays the reformers as God's chosen people, the children of Israel, struggling against the pharaoh, the Duke of Savoy. Farel, Froment, and Viret appear in prominent vignettes—lone, David-like figures prevailing against the Catholic Savoyard Goliath. The author tells with unusual rhetorical restraint how allies from Berne delayed coming to their aid. By contrast, sympathizers from Neuchâtel emerge as heroic allies, rallying to send reinforcements to their Genevan "brothers" (65). Their courage reinforced by God, they overcome more than four hundred of the enemy while their own losses numbered seven dead and two wounded. Two Savoyard priests exemplify base cowardice by breaking into the place sheltering the two wounded men and cutting their throats.

The author of *The War and Deliverance* [*La guerre et délivrance*] shows little concern about gender. Women are portrayed as passive victims and are generally absent from the heroic accounts. However, as if to emphasize the disproportion in courage between the two sides, the author offers this notable but anonymous exception: "A Swiss woman defeated four Savoyards. What would we expect from the men?" (66). The implications of that rhetorical question are left to the reader. The authorial first-person voice speaks only once and identifies itself as a man, as he apologizes for his inability to convey the cruelty and malice the reformers confronted: "[I]n short, it is impossible for a merchant such as I am to be able to write about it adequately" (39). The language of the work is energetic, at times coarse, and as confrontational as the events it describes. In that respect, it is similar to the other works produced by the reformers during those years, in many cases works by the very men it portrays: Farel, Viret, and Froment, for example, as well as the *Very Useful Epistle*. However, the authorship of *The War and Deliverance of the City of Geneva* remains an unresolved question. It was not until 1881 that Swiss scholar Albert Rilliet, in his edition of the work, challenged the authenticity of the "merchant" and argued that the work was by same author who later wrote the *Very Useful Epistle*, Marie Dentière. Unconvinced by the reference to the merchant-author in the work, Rilliet rejected the hypothesis that her husband, reformer Antoine Froment—who was a merchant of sorts—authored the work. He based his argument on similarities of language and style that he perceived between *The War and Deliverance* and the *Epistle*. He provides cross-references after several fragments of the *Epistle*, sending the reader to places in *The War and Deliverance* where he sensed echoes, but he does not specify the stylistic affinities that led him to his conclusion. Those cross-references alone do not provide convincing proof for Rilliet's assertion that Marie Dentière wrote both works. Guillaume Farel, for example, was well-known for his thundering sermons and his fierce invective.[17] His colleagues who eventually welcomed him in Neuchâtel—home of the valiant heroes depicted in *The War and Deliverance*—shared rhetorical traits as well as doctrinal beliefs with the reformers preaching and writing in Geneva. Did they also bring reinforcement to the chronicle that praised their courageous effort? *The War and Deliverance* offers a valuable account of the years when Marie Dentière first lived in Geneva, but the identity of its author remains for now a mystery.

There is no doubt, however, that Marie Dentière played an active role in the events of those years, becoming an outspoken participant in the reform movement, preaching her opposition to religious celibacy, and advocating women's pastoral role in the new church. In August, 1535, accompanying Farel and Viret, she invaded the Poor Clares' convent in Geneva, urging the nuns to leave their order and renounce celibacy. The only published contemporary report of that speech was written by another woman, Jeanne de Jussie, eventual abbess in that order. Looking back on the events of those days, she draws a colorful portrait of her adversary: "In that company was a monkess, false abbess, wrinkled, and with a diabolical tongue, having husband and children, named Marie Dentière of Picardy, who meddled in preaching and in perverting people of devotion." Jussie introduces Dentière as a nun who had betrayed her vow of chastity and violated the injunction against women's speech. She reports that the scandalized nuns rebuffed Dentière, calling her a "disavowed monk and poisoned tongue," but that she persisted in preaching to them. Jussie gives this record of that speech and the reaction it evoked:

> "Ah, poor creatures, if only you knew how good it was to be next to a handsome husband, and how God thinks it pleasing. I was for a long time in that darkness and hypocrisy where you are, but God alone made me recognize the abuse of my wretched life, and I came to the true light of truth, considering that I lived in regret, because in those religions there is only cant, mental corruption and idleness, and so, without delay I took from the treasury of the abbey almost five hundred ducats, and I left that unhappiness, and, thanks to God alone, I

17. See Skenazi's comparison of Farel's and Dentière's styles in "Marie Dentière et la prédication des femmes." Francis Higman compares the styles of Viret, Farel, and Marcourt to that of Calvin in *The Style of John Calvin in His French Polemical Treatises*, 170–76.

have five beautiful children, and I live a salutary life." The nuns were horrified by her false and erroneous words, and they spat on her with loathing. [Dentière continued] "Ah! false hypocrites, you scorn the word of God because you are not with Him. We know well the kind of life you lead. Your enlightened sister has told us about your dissolute and diabolical life. The poor girl could not endure it." Saying those abominable words, the wretched woman tried to charm the sisters, and the others tried to drag some of them outside. (238–39)[18]

Written years after the antagonistic encounter it describes, the account of the speech reveals stereotypical notions about women, convent life, and marriage, notions that colored Reformation polemic on both sides. Jussie portrays Dentière accusing the nuns in the convent of leading a dissolute life, a common charge leveled by the reformers against Catholic religious orders. However, she also shapes Dentière's "abominable" words in order to convey and reinforce a notion held by Catholics that reformers were too vulnerable to the pleasures of the flesh. The reference to Dentière's intimacy with her handsome husband and the children who resulted from their union gives an earthy, erotic tone to her appeal, one that certainly would have shocked in that place of cloistered, celibate women. Jussie conveys a biased view of the reformers' defense of marriage and rejection of celibacy.[19] She also portrays Dentière as admitting to having stolen money from her convent. While hostile, Jeanne de Jussie's rendering of the incident nevertheless gives a memorable vignette of Dentière's active participation in the events leading to the reformers' victory in Geneva. Jussie conveys the rhetorical verve and feisty manner in Dentière's words that the *Very Useful Epistle* and the later preface to Calvin's sermon on Timothy confirm. Her portrait also shows Dentière as an outspoken partner of Farel and Viret in their proselytizing efforts—a working alliance that was not to develop harmoniously.

THE REFORMATION IN FRANCE

To appreciate Marie Dentière's *Epistle*, we need to place the events in Geneva in the broader context of reform in France during the 1530s. Dentière ad-

18. Jussie, *Petite chronique*. It is unlikely that Dentière had been, as Jussie says, an abbess before leaving the convent. For a broader view of French convents in Dentière's time, see Blaisdell, "Religion, Gender, and Class."

19. Elisabeth M. Wengler has analyzed Jussie's account of Dentière's visit as well as the broader role each woman played in the history of Reformation Geneva in "Women, Religion, and Reform in Sixteenth-Century Geneva"; see especially chs. 3 and 4, in particular, pp. 99–101. See also Lazard, "Deux soeurs ennemies, Marie Dentière et Jeanne de Jussie."

dressed the *Epistle* to Marguerite de Navarre, who remained the visible pa-
troness of the French evangelical reform, although her power to protect its
members had begun to diminish by the time the *Epistle* appeared. The public
would have known that Marguerite was the author of *The Mirror of the Sinful
Soul*, a long mystical poem published in 1533; they would have known that
the University of Paris theologians had objected to the book, placing it on a
list of censured titles for that year.[20] Marguerite's brother the king had inter-
vened; royal pressure was exerted, and the theologian censors retreated. The
Epistle foregrounds those two women, one appealing passionately to the
other, and its many references to events in France remind us that the efforts
for reform inside and outside of France were closely intertwined. Many of the
people working for religious reform in Switzerland had, like Dentière, left
France searching for a safer haven. Exiles, they maintained their hopes and
efforts that the Reformed Church would one day flourish in their homeland.
There was Calvin, of course, born in Picardy in 1509; but well before he arrived in Geneva in 1536, the preachers of the reformed faith in the French-
speaking Swiss cantons were often French. Farel was prominent among
them, as were both of Marie Dentière's husbands. It is not surprising that
those expatriates maintained frequent contacts with advocates of reform remaining in France and tried actively to support them. Antoine Marcourt, another native of Picardy, came to Switzerland via Lyon and became the first
pastor of the Reformed Church of Neuchâtel in 1530.[21] His actions were to
have a dramatic impact on the course of events in his native country.

October 1534, marks a turning point in the history of religious reform in
France. Before that date, Francis I had been fairly tolerant toward the evangelical reformers. Encouraged by his sister Marguerite, he had often in-
tervened to protect people accused of heresy by the Sorbonne and the
Parlement of Paris, the powers of Catholic orthodoxy in France. There were
promising signs for the evangelical church. In early 1534 Francis was under-
taking negotiations with several German princes in an effort to bring about a
peaceful resolution of religious differences. However, Francis did not tolerate reformist activity that threatened public order in his kingdom. On October 18, 1534, copies of placards or posters that were considered blasphemous
in their attack on the Catholic Mass appeared widely in Paris and in several
provincial cities. Reports claimed that one of them had even been affixed to
the door of Francis's private chambers. The posters had been composed and
printed in Neuchâtel and were the work of Marcourt. Public reaction ranged

---

20. Marguerite de Navarre, *Le miroir de l'âme pécheresse.*

21. Berthoud, *Antoine Marcourt.*

from indignation to hysteria. Foreigners in Paris were suspect. A Flemish merchant was lynched by a crowd that thought he was German—and therefore a Lutheran. Official reaction was immediate. Harsh persecution pursued the French reformers as it never had before. By the end of November several dissenters and suspected heretics had been executed. Shaken by the audacious affront to his authority and the threat of worse to come, Francis abruptly withdrew his support from the reformers. In January 1535 more placards appeared, along with printed pamphlets, and the king banned all printing. On a public day of penance in late January, Francis I walked in a procession, and six more people were burned. A royal edict published the names of seventy-three "Lutherans" who had gone into hiding and demanded that they turn themselves in. Among those who fled France in the aftermath of those events was the young John Calvin, who sought refuge at Marguerite's castle in Nérac before proceeding to Italy and eventually to Switzerland. With the change in royal attitude after the Placards Affair, the Faculty of Theology and the French Parlement, which had often been frustrated by Francis in their efforts to suppress the evangelical reformers, regained power and influence, becoming his ally in the effort to restore order.[22]

THE CONTEXT OF THE *VERY USEFUL EPISTLE*

In 1537 Antoine Froment was named deacon at Thonon in the Chablais, on the south shore of Lake Geneva, but he and his wife remained closely associated with the unfolding events in Geneva. Urged by Farel to remain in the city, Calvin quickly became a prominent force in shaping the role of the Reformed Church there. More severe in his notion of Christian conduct than Farel, Calvin proposed strict disciplines that alienated many Genevans, even many who were supporters of the reformed religion. They resisted Calvin's attempts to make everyone sign his *Confession of Faith* under threat of exile. Calvin and Farel resisted in turn the Council of Two Hundred's efforts to impose ordinances that would make their liturgical practices conform to those of Lausanne and Berne. Calvin and Farel refused to budge from their insis-

22. A good account of Francis's attitude toward the Reform appears in Knecht, *Renaissance Warrior and Patron: The Reign of Francis I;* see the chapter entitled "Humanism and Heresy." For the Placards Affair, see Knecht, *Renaissance Warrior,* 313–21; Eire, *War against the Idols,* 189–93; and Hillerbrand, ed., *Oxford Encyclopedia of the Reformation,* vol. 1. Higman gives the text of the placards in *La diffusion de la Réforme en France, 1520–1565,* 72–75. For a thorough recent study of the Reformation in France, see Crouzet, *La genèse de la Réforme française, 1520–1560.* See also Defaux, "1534, 17–18 October: The Posting of Violent Anti-Catholic Placards in France's Main Cities and on the Very Door of Francis I's Room Launches a Period of Systematic Repression," in Hollier et al., *A New History of French Literature,* 162–67.

tence on ecclesiastical independence. The affair became a stand-off in the week before Easter in 1538 when Calvin and Farel refused to celebrate the Lord's Supper under the rules of the ordinances. The council responded by banishing the two ministers. Farel returned to Neuchâtel, and Calvin went to Basel and later to Strasbourg. Marcourt was brought from Neuchâtel to fill one of the vacancies created by their exile. The affair caused alarm far beyond Geneva. Froment later reported that when Marguerite de Navarre heard of the banishment and wanted to learn how it had come about, she turned to Marie Dentière, whom she apparently already knew fairly well:

> The Queen of Navarre wanted to learn from a friend [*commere*] of hers, named Marie Dentière, from Tournai, wife of Froment, the first woman in our time expelled because of the Gospel, having left her abbey and monastery, now living in Geneva—wanted to know her news and learn how this dispute had come about and why the ministers of God's word in Geneva had been expelled.[23]

Dentière responded by sending to Marguerite the *Very Useful Epistle* [*Epistre tres utile*], apparently before it appeared in Geneva in April, 1539.[24]

What was the nature of the relationship between Marie Dentière and Marguerite de Navarre? The word *commere* in the sixteenth century meant "godmother" or, more particularly, the relationship between a child's godmother and its parents.[25] Since, in the Mazarine copy of the *Epistle*, Dentière refers to her daughter as "my little daughter your goddaughter [*fillolle*]," both she and Froment imply that Marguerite de Navarre was the godmother of that little girl, one of the children from Dentière's marriage to Simon Robert. It is not known whether Marguerite was present at the daughter's baptism, and it is not clear when and how the French king's sister met Dentière. It is possible that Dentière spent some time in France after leaving her convent in Tournai and before arriving in Strasbourg and that, as part of the evangelical community that Marguerite aided, she would have met the queen. Communication was frequent between Marguerite and the French in Strasbourg, some of whom traveled on evangelical missions. In the years between 1525 and 1539, Marguerite de Navarre had several opportunities either to encounter Marie Dentière in person or to keep informed of her activities through mutual friends. In a letter to Farel in Strasbourg written from France

23. Transcribed from Froment's unpublished papers in Herminjard, *Correspondance,* 5: 295, n. 2 (no. 785).

24. Dentière, *Epistre tres utile.* See Kemp and Desrosiers-Bonin, "Marie d'Ennetières et la petite grammaire hébraïque," 121, n. 17.

25. According to the context, *commere* could also mean a female gossip, but that denotation is clearly not applicable in Froment's report.

in 1526, Gérard Roussel tells of presenting a "part of his work" to "the Duchess." Marguerite de Navarre was then still the Duchess of Alençon. The work was presumably the translation of the Bible into French that Lefèvre d'Etaples and other French exiles had undertaken together. Roussel reports that Marguerite accepted the excerpt with pleasure, and he urges Farel and "our brother Simon" to continue the task. Simon was Marie Dentière's husband, Simon Robert. Roussel asks Farel to give his greetings to "the sisters" or wives of the Strasbourg pastors and their French comrades. It is easy to imagine that Roussel's conversation with Marguerite about the Strasbourg community included news of Simon Robert's wife.[26] When Lefèvre d'Etaples returned to France, he spent the remaining years until his death in 1536 at Marguerite's court in Nérac. Once the Strasbourg French group dispersed, the Queen of Navarre continued to follow with interest the paths taken by those men and women. In the *Epistle*, Dentière addresses Marguerite with conventional formulas of respect, but she does not shrink from sharply criticizing people close to Marguerite and attacking positions that the Queen would have recognized as her own.

While Marguerite is the designated recipient of the *Epistle*, Dentière clearly intended a wider audience for her work. Those targeted readers would include people she criticizes and attacks: the authorities in Geneva who had made Calvin and Farel leave, the powerful hierarchy of the Catholic Church, believers in reform who stayed in the Catholic Church, and members of the French court who tolerated or supported them. She directs her message as well to the people she encourages: the faithful already committed to reform and candidates for conversion in both France and French-speaking Switzerland. Prominent among them are her female readers:

> Not only for you, my Lady, did I wish to write this letter, but also to give courage to other women detained in captivity, so that they might not fear being expelled from their homelands, away from their relatives and friends, as I was, for the word of God. And principally for the poor [a3v] little women wanting to know and understand the truth, who do not know what path, what way to take, in order that from now on they not be internally tormented and afflicted, but rather that they be joyful, consoled and led to follow the truth, which is the Gospel of Jesus Christ.

Dentière makes Marguerite a part of that community of women. Her name on the title page would draw more attention to the work and give it more authority. Dentière is careful to point out in the opening dedicatory letter that

---

26. Herminjard, *Correspondance*, 1: 439 (no. 178); 1: 449 (no. 182); and 1: 457–61 (no. 184).

Marguerite is her model, a woman who dared to articulate and to publish dissident religious beliefs.

The *Epistle* asks the queen's support for the reformed religion and expresses the hope that women will no longer be considered inadequate as readers of Scripture. Following the dedicatory address to Marguerite is a section entitled "A Defense of Women," a vigorous rebuttal of misogynist discourse that argues for an active role for women in the church by citing female biblical authorities, strong women from both the New Testament and the Old. The body of the *Epistle* itself is a long polemical attack on those whom Marie Dentière and her associates perceived as enemies of the true reformed religion. While attacking the enemy, she presents her own positions on the most important theological questions at issue in the Reformation. At the same time, she defends with passionate and indignant conviction women's equality before God and their right to be theologians and teachers.

Like all of the works attributed to Marie Dentière, the *Epistle* has a complicated publication history. The small octavo volume included on its title page the admonition: "Read and then judge" and carried the false notice that it had been printed in Antwerp, at the shop of Martin L'Empereur.[27] That claim did not stop the Geneva Council from raiding the shop of Jean Girard, a printer whose sympathies for Farel and Calvin were well-known. The *Epistle's* biting criticism of those who had caused their expulsion was more than the council could tolerate. They arrested Girard and seized the remaining copies of the *Epistle* found there. Antoine Froment went before the Geneva Council to protest the seizure of his wife's *Epistle* and request that the copies be released to him. He excused Girard's false indication of the Antwerp printer, saying that Antoine Marcourt, who was by then established in the Geneva church, had often given similar false information when he published in Neuchâtel. The confiscated books were held for some time, but they eventually disappeared, presumably destroyed. However, enough copies had already been circulated that the efforts to suppress the *Epistle* were only partly successful.[28]

The work created a significant stir. Early reaction to it, even among those who shared its sentiments, was mixed. Some expressed unwillingness

---

27. See Kemp, "L'épigraphe 'Lisez et puis jugez.'"

28. According to Dufour, the book's publication resulted in an ordinance preventing any book from being published without prior inspection and approval by the Council. See his *Notice bibliographique* for a brief biography of Girard (78–85) and for details of the *Epistle's* confiscation (155–59). Higman records that the publication led to a lawsuit for Girard: see *Piety and the People*, 167–68. Froment's argument to the Geneva Council is recorded in Herminjard, *Correspondance*, 5: 302–3, n. 18.

to believe that it had been written by a woman. The Berne Councillors inquired about "Froment's book," and the Lausanne pastor Beatus Comte reported to them about it in a document dated August 26, 1539:

> It is not against Holy Scripture, nor against our religion and faith. But it is true that it has certain articles that can be misinterpreted by the wicked and malicious, and that it is not appropriate for the current times. Furthermore, because the title announces that a woman (who has no business prophesying in the Church) dictated and composed it, and because that is not true—for that reason he advises suppressing the book and thinks it not worth a squabble. It is decided that at the same time the judgment be announced to Froment in a letter.[29]

Comte's rejection of Marie Dentière's role as author can be understood in the early modern climate that refused women a public voice. He may have concluded that Froment was the author because he could not imagine a woman in that capacity. Froment had already played a prominent role in the reformers' takeover of Geneva and was well known for preaching publicly on the Place Molard. Comte may have noticed the word *froment* (wheat) slipped into the final page of the *Epistle* as a punning allusion to Dentière's husband and his role in the project. Even though the Reformation defended marriage for its pastors and encouraged wives to support their husbands' ministries, its leaders, like Beatus Comte, were not ready to acknowledge that a woman could publish a work of reformed doctrine or that a pastor could collaborate on such a project with his wife. Froment's investment in the *Epistle* is clear from his plea before the Geneva Council for release of the confiscated copies. He defends the *Epistle's* worthiness and offers to vouch for it himself if his wife's assurance of its orthodoxy is not sufficient. The contested volume clearly expressed doctrinal and political positions that the couple shared. The degree to which Froment may have contributed to parts of the *Epistle* is not clear, but such collaboration would not be unusual among the French reformers. From the days in Strasbourg when translation of the Bible into French was, as Roussel described it, "our work," collaboration was standard practice for spreading the word of the reformed religion. Whatever his role may have been, Froment did not hesitate to attribute the *Epistle* to his wife, Marie Dentière.

In spite of the efforts of the Geneva Council, copies of the *Epistle* survived and were circulated. Froment had removed some four hundred copies from Girard's shop before the remaining volumes were confiscated. Only two copies are known to have survived, one in the library of the Musée His-

---

29. Ibid., 5: 333, n. 2–3 (no. 796).

torique de la Réformation at the University of Geneva (D Den 1) and the other in the Bibliothèque Mazarine in Paris (Rés 25543).[30]

Aside from Jeanne de Jussie's report, the *Epistle* affair, and a letter of Calvin's to which we shall return, we get only rare glimpses of Marie Dentière from contemporary sources. We have to glean hints of her whereabouts from references to her husband, Froment, and *uxor Frumenti*, Froment's wife. While we cannot assume that the life of the husband always parallels that of the wife, contemporary reports of Froment's activities imply that she was actively involved in his work and even an important influence on him—a bad influence, according to those reports. The couple's relationship with the leaders of the Reformed Church in Geneva and the nearby Swiss cities was frequently troubled, and Marie Dentière was sometimes implicated in criticism of her husband's behavior. In a letter to Calvin in Strasbourg written some six months before the *Epistle* appeared, Farel wrote, "You know how Froment, a very imprudent man who cares little about the church, behaves with his wife—unless it is she who makes him behave that way."[31] In 1540, Farel again complained about Dentière's influence on her husband, making a pun on his name, which means "wheat" in French:

> Our Froment, first in his home by following his wife's example, has degenerated into a weed, and we would have expected nothing less of them, since they have such a bad reputation among the lovers of sects to whom they had been hostile. They seem to behave, not like soldiers of Christ who defend wholeheartedly the cause of the Gospel so that they may convert others to it, but like enemies, conspirators who look out for themselves.[32]

In 1540 Froment was appointed pastor at Massongy, a village between Thonon and Geneva. Froment's fellow pastors in the Chablais complained about his business dealings, finding them inappropriate for a minister of the Church. Their complaints mention his wife. In 1541 they wrote to the Berne Council complaining about Froment's activities as a merchant.

> You have known that Antoine Froment was, from the beginning, involved in many business deals and that he did many things unworthy

30. Higman, *Piety and the People*, 168. For a detailed analysis of the differences between the two volumes, see Kemp and Desrosiers-Bonin, "Marie d'Ennetières et la petite grammaire hébraïque."

31. Herminjard, *Correspondance*, 5: 151 (no. 752).

32. Ibid., 6: 173–74 (no. 847). Froment's colleagues, and even he and his wife, occasionally punned on the meaning of his name. Here Farel calls Froment *Triticeus* (wheat in Latin) and observes that the "wheat has gone to weed."

of a minister of God's word. While in Geneva he was more a merchant than a preacher, when he spent the whole week conducting business and, with his wife, publicly ran a shop. And on Sundays he preached the word of God. Besides the many other scandals he caused, he purchased a lot of oil in town and in the villages around Thonon and became an oil merchant. . . . We consider him a real Demas, seeing how avidly he embraced the love of the world.[33]

The letter goes on to accuse Froment of hoarding and speculating on wine and—even worse—of being resolutely unrepentant when castigated by them.

Calvin, at least at the end of his life, had a more indulgent view of Froment's double career than did the pastors in the Chablais. In his farewell speech to the Company of Pastors in 1564, one month before he died, he recalled fondly his early years in Geneva: "To be sure, there was good master William [Farel] and also blind Courault. Moreover there was Master Antoine Saulnier and that fine preacher Froment, who, having put aside his apron, mounted the pulpit and then climbed back down to his store where he would gab, thus preaching a double sermon."[34] Froment's fellow pastors at the time, however, continued to take a dim view of the way he handled his pastoral obligations and related financial affairs. In January 1542 the Council of Berne, Froment's superiors, concluded an investigation that found some improprieties in his ministry, but he retained his post at Massongy, at least for a time.

In the summer of 1542, Froment traveled to Lyon while Francis I and his sister were in residence there and succeeded in meeting with Marguerite. Upon his return to Geneva, he reported to Calvin. His accounts of his conversation with the queen conveyed an air of self-importance that both irritated and amused Calvin, who wrote as follows to Pierre Viret on August 19:

Froment returned lately from Lyon. He reports that the Queen of Navarre is at present even better disposed than ever she was; and he even gives the assurance in her own language, for he was admitted to familiar converse in an interview with her. Howsoever you are aware that we must not rashly hold every word that the messenger utters to be strictly true; for he is so carried away by the honor which has been put upon him in having been admitted to an interview with the Queen,

33. Ibid., 6: 401–4 (no. 927). See also Meylan, *Silhouettes du XVIᵉ siècle,* 97. In 2 Timothy 4:10, Paul complains about one of his disciples: "For Demas, in love with this present world, has deserted me and gone to Thessalonica."

34. Calvin, *Ioannis Calvini opera quae supersunt omniae,* vol. 9, cols. 891–94. English translation in Monter, *Calvin's Geneva,* 95.

that he seems to me to have lost the small remnant of common sense which he still possessed. To say nought of other absurdities, when he mentioned that the Queen wished me to write to her, he thought proper to dictate at the same time the subject-matter; and, having but little confidence in my judgment, he forbade my writing and sending away my letter unless previously read and revised by himself. He has spread a report through the whole city that he was very near preaching before the King himself. There are a thousand silly statements of this sort. Do not think, however, that all he says is false; he heard part of what he says from the Queen or her ministers. But these artful courtiers, when they get hold of a simple-minded individual, abuse his credulity for their own advantage or amusement.[35]

It is not clear whether Marie Dentière accompanied her husband on that trip to Lyon to meet with the woman Froment called her *commere* and to whom she had addressed her *Epistle*. However, Froment's privileged access to Marguerite probably was owed to, or at least facilitated by, his wife's earlier connection with her, one that pre-dated by several years Dentiere's marriage to Froment. However, this is another one of the many glimpses into Marie Dentière's world where she remains an intriguing absence.

The tone of Calvin's letter makes it clear that he dismissed and ridiculed Froment's efforts to act as his emissary to the French royal family, and it also reveals criticism of the royal court. Later, relations between Calvin and Marguerite were to degenerate. Some partisans of reform judged that she had gone into a contemplative withdrawal and a corresponding indifference toward outward forms that permitted her to remain within the Catholic Church while following her own personal faith. Calvin excoriated such behavior in his 1544 treatise, *Against the Nicodemites*. In April 1545, he wrote a letter to Marguerite defending his attack on the Spiritual Libertines, a group whom she had supported.[36] The record of Marguerite's last years before her death in 1549 indicates that her apparent retreat alarmed others sympathetic to the reform movement. Rabelais dedicated his 1546 *Third Book of Pantagruel* to "the spirit of the Queen of Navarre," whom he addressed as "Abstract, rav-

35. Herminjard, *Correspondance*, 8: 106–7 (no. 1149); Calvin, *Letters of John Calvin*, 342–43.

36. See *Excuse de Jehan Calvin à Messieurs les Nicodémites* in Calvin, *Three French Treatises*, introduction, 21–26 and 131–53; and *Letters of John Calvin*, 1: 453–58. For Calvin's letter to Marguerite, see *Ioannis Calvini opera*, vol. 12, no. 634, col. 64–68. Thysell studies the relationship between Calvin and Marguerite in *The Pleasures of Discernment: Marguerite de Navarre as Theologian*. Reid argues convincingly that Marguerite continued until her death to engage in behind-the-scenes politics to defend the evangelical cause; see "King's Sister, Queen of Dissent," 512–69.

ished and ecstatic spirit," urging her to leave her divine abode and return to earth. We have no trace of further interaction between Marguerite and Marie Dentière.

Calvin's tone becomes derisive in 1546 when he records a subsequent encounter with Marie Dentière herself. Here we see an even more audacious Dentière than the woman who exhorted the Poor Clares to leave their convent. Now she is determined to reach a wider, more public audience. She is once again reviling the ministers of Geneva, but now Calvin is their leader. Where Jeanne de Jussie had portrayed her as a comrade of Farel's and Viret's, here she is alone, alienated from the very people whom she had supported. Yet she remains undaunted. Seven years after writing her *Epistle,* she does not hesitate to challenge even Calvin, who relates his encounter with her in a letter written to Farel:

> I'm going to tell you a funny story. Froment's wife came here recently; in all the taverns, at almost all the street corners, she began to harangue against long garments. When she knew that it had gotten back to me, she excused herself, laughing, and said that either we were dressed indecently, with great offense to the church, or that you taught in error when you said that false prophets could be recognized by their long garments.

Calvin argues with Dentière, denying her accusations that he and his associates are like the scribes evoked in Luke 20:45 "who want to walk about in long robes." Calvin concludes: "Feeling pressured, she complained about our tyranny, that it was no longer permitted for just anyone to chatter on about anything at all. I treated the woman as I should have."[37]

It would be hard to find two more unlikely allies than Jeanne de Jussie, the abbess of the Poor Clares' convent, and John Calvin. Yet, in spite of their opposing positions on the Reform, they offer similar portraits of Marie Dentière: an outspoken woman stepping out of her proper place, transgressing the conventions of speech and space that society had imposed on her sex. In Jussie's portrait, she enters the Poor Clares' convent not as a woman wanting to take the vows of the order but as a siren calling for women to abandon those vows and emerge into a life of divinely sanctioned marital pleasure. Eleven years later, she has become even bolder. She goes to the most public

---

37. Calvin, *Letters of John Calvin,* 2: 70–71. I have modified Bonnet's translation. The original letter, in Latin, dated September 1, 1546, can be found in *Ioannis Calvini opera,* vol. 12, no. 824, cols. 377–78. Head comments on the encounter in "The Religion of the *Femmelettes*," 161–62. See also Thompson, *John Calvin and the Daughters of Sarah,* 42n.

of urban spaces, a woman daring to preach in the taverns and on the street corners, places traditionally frequented by men.[38] She is a woman unafraid to confront even Calvin, to criticize his behavior and accuse him and his associates of tyranny and error. From the viewpoints of Jussie and Calvin, she is unruly and, therefore, an object of contempt and ridicule. Calvin's anecdote is particularly derisive because he introduces it as a joke. But as Natalie Zemon Davis has noted, "women on top" are often the object of comedy.[39]

As witnesses, both the Poor Clares' abbess and the Geneva minister wrote with a clear bias. However, Calvin adds a detail that points to a different attitude toward Marie Dentière. After her encounter with him, he tells us: "She immediately proceeded to the widow of Michael, who gave her a hospitable reception, sharing with her not only her table but her bed, because she maligned the ministers." We do not know any details about Michael's widow. Calvin's remark suggests, however, that she shared Dentière's criticism of him and would have recorded a more sympathetic view of her than either Jussie's or Calvin's.

It is not surprising that the two contemporary hostile vignettes of Marie Dentière portray her preaching. The public role of women in church teaching was a highly charged issue among the early reformers, generating frequent, often passionate commentary. Henricus Cornelius Agrippa (1486–1535), in his *Declamation on the Nobility and Preeminence of the Female Sex*, composed in 1509 and circulated in manuscript before being published in Antwerp in 1529, criticized women's exclusion:

> They are excluded also from preaching the word of God, in contradiction to Scripture where the Holy Spirit, by the mouth of Joel, has promised them: "Your daughters will also prophesy." In this spirit women taught publicly in the time of the Apostles, as we know from Anna, wife of Simeon, from the daughters of Philip, and from Priscilla, wife of Aquila. But our modern legislators are of such bad faith that they have made null and void the commandment of God, they have decreed according to their own traditions that women, however otherwise naturally eminent and of remarkable nobility, are inferior in status to all men.[40]

---

38. Tlustly gives a good view of the culture of German public taverns in "Gender and Alcohol Use in Early Modern Augsburg."

39. See Davis, *Society and Culture in Early Modern France*, 124–51. See also Stallybrass, "Patriarchal Territories: The Body Enclosed"; and Parker, *Literary Fat Ladies: Rhetoric, Gender, and Property*, 8–35.

40. Agrippa, *Declamation on the Nobility and Preeminence of the Female Sex*, 95.

Reforming the church raised the possibility of reversing the tradition of misogyny that prevented women from preaching. However, the new religious leaders often proved to be just as intransigent as their predecessors, particularly when it concerned admitting women into public ministerial roles.[41] One of the central points of Dentière's letter to Marguerite de Navarre is that women should be able to teach the gospel to one another, that they are as worthy and capable as men to do so. Natalie Zemon Davis has proposed that Dentière's claim to address herself only to other women was a "modest fiction."[42] Several passages in the *Epistle* suggest that the fiction barely veiled her conviction that women were worthy to preach to both men and women and just as fit for the task as were men. Calvin's letter confirms that she acted on that conviction.

Dentière was not alone in criticizing Calvin and the Reformed Church leaders. Her husband's preaching and outspoken criticism of them eventually led to his removal from the ministry. In 1548, Froment preached a sermon attacking the church leaders of Germany, Constance, Berne, and Geneva, accusing them of making private gain from their ministries and losing sight of the spirit of the Reformed Church, charges reminiscent of the criticisms directed earlier against Froment by Farel. A court case followed, and the Berne Council had Froment removed from his post as pastor of Massongy. Froment left the official ministry and from then on made his living as a secretary. The Council of Geneva assigned him to assist François Bonivard in producing his *Chronicles of Geneva*. Froment would eventually compose his own chronicle of the city's reformation, *The Actions and Wondrous Feats of the City of Geneva Newly Converted to the Gospel*.[43] Charges of dissolute behavior brought against him in 1561 are murky at best. Marie Dentière's reactions to those events are not known.

---

41. The literature on women's role as teachers in the Reformed Church is extensive. For the situation most relevant to Marie Dentière, see Douglass, *Women, Freedom, and Calvin,* 83–107; and Thompson, *John Calvin and the Daughters of Sarah,* 187–226. Thompson's bibliography is a valuable resource on the question. For more general comments, see the chapter entitled "City Women and Religious Change," in Davis, *Society and Culture,* 65–95; Blaisdell, "The Matrix of Reform: Women in the Lutheran and Calvinist Movements"; Wiesner, "Women's Defense of Their Public Role"; and Head, "The Religion of the *Femmelettes.*" Maclean provides a brief background for women's disqualification from preaching in the Church in *The Renaissance Notion of Woman,* 18.

42. Davis, *Society and Culture,* 82–83.

43. Fromment, *Les actes et gestes merveilleux de la cité de Genève nouvellement convertie à l'Evangile.* On the end of Froment's ministry, see Meylan, *Silhouettes du XVIᵉ siècle,* 100–105. A new critical edition of Bonivard has begun to appear; see Bonivard, *Chroniques de Genève.*

PREFACE TO CALVIN'S SERMON

The animosity recorded in Calvin's letter to Farel about Dentière's behavior makes all the more interesting a rare edition of Calvin's *Sermon on the modesty of women in their dress* published in 1561. Calvin preached a series of fifty-four sermons on 1 Timothy in 1554–55; these were published for the first time in Geneva by Conrad Badius in 1561, the year of Dentière's death. Soon thereafter, one of the sermons, the seventeenth, on 1 Timothy (2:9–11), was published separately in two editions.[44] Both editions carried a preface, addressed "to the Christian reader" and signed only with the initials M.D. Those initials, recalling the initials of the "Christian woman from Tournai" on the Geneva copy of the *Very Useful Epistle,* have led scholars to identify the author of the preface as Marie Dentière. The word *froment* (wheat) at the end of both the preface and the *Epistle* serves as another link between the two texts, a punning signature relating both works to Antoine Froment and his wife, Marie Dentière.

What would have led Marie Dentière to introduce Calvin's sermon? It is vexing that we know so little about her later life, the fifteen years between her public encounter with Calvin and her death in 1561. Does the preface indicate that she and Calvin reconciled after their hostile encounter? The history of the reformers in French-speaking Switzerland shows that disapproval and reproach often colored their interactions, but that the discord they experienced did not stop them ultimately from working together on the common cause of reform. Calvin and Farel themselves had an often rocky history, what Francis Higman calls "altogether a very curious relationship," arising in part from Calvin's "almost tortured sensitivity."[45] However, Calvin's farewell letter to the Company of Pastors in 1564 showed that he was capable of mellowing toward Farel, "good Master William," and even toward "that fine preacher Froment." Perhaps his heart had softened, too, toward Marie Dentière, or perhaps the two had reconciled for other reasons.

---

44. See Peter and Gilmont, *Bibliotheca Calviniana,* vol. 2, *Ecrits théologiques, littéraires et juridiques, 1555–1564,* entry 61/1 (Lunel, Bibliothèque municipale, Fonds Médard) and entry 61/23 (Geneva, Musée Historique de la Reformation). Hornus and Peter describe the Lunel volume (*Les conditions et vertus requises en la femme fidèle et bonne mesnagere: contenues au xxxi. chapitre des Prouerbes de Salomon. Mis en forme de Cantique, par Theodore de Besze. Plus, un Sermon de la modestie des Femmes en leurs habillemens, par. M. Iean Calvin. Outre, plusieurs chansons spirituelles, en Musique.* M.D.LXI.) and give excerpts of the preface (54–55) in "*Calviniana rarissima* du Fonds Jean-Louis Médard à la Bibliothèque municipale de Lunel." I thank Mme Denise Rouger of the Bibliothèque municipale in Lunel for graciously giving me access to the library's volume.

45. Higman analyzes a little-known letter that Calvin wrote to Farel from Strasbourg in December 1539, just eight months after the appearance of Marie Dentière's *Epistle.* The letter is enlightening about the nature of Calvin's relationship with Farel. See his "Calvin and Farel."

Another possible explanation is that a shared concern about the future of the reformed religion brought Calvin and Dentière together, at least in print, in spite of their personal antipathy. Recent events in France would have been cause for alarm among the Swiss reformers. In the late 1550s, in spite of King Henry II's repressive measures against heresy, Calvinism spread in France and attracted nobles as well as working-class converts. The growth of the reformed religion met with consternation. On September 4, 1557, an angry crowd in Paris broke into a house on the rue Saint-Jacques and disrupted a Reformed Church celebration of the Lord's Supper. Several hundred Huguenots—the name had just begun to be applied to them—were present, including some noblewomen. Word spread that the meeting had been an occasion of ritual debauchery. At least nine of those arrested were eventually executed. Opponents continued to spread tales that the Calvinists were morally corrupt and sexually dissolute.[46] Calvin's sermon on modesty would have provided a good weapon to counter that propaganda, as well as a reminder to his followers living in France of the importance of sober behavior. Meanwhile, Gaspard de Coligny had become Admiral of France and was already a close advisor of King Charles IX and his mother, Catherine de' Medici, Henri II's widowed queen. He was to become the respected leader of the Huguenot party in France and would be one of the first to die in the infamous St. Bartholomew's Day Massacre in 1572. In 1561, Coligny acquired a new personal chaplain, Jean-Raymond Merlin. Merlin, a long-standing associate of Calvin, pastor and professor of Hebrew in Lausanne, had married the daughter of Marie Dentière and Simon Robert, the young girl, apparent goddaughter of Marguerite de Navarre, who had sent a Hebrew grammar to the young Jeanne d'Albret in 1539. It is plausible that Merlin asked his mother-in-law to write a preface to Calvin's sermon, thus fostering in 1561 a French publication that would work against the image of Huguenots as lubricious libertines.[47] In that same year, Marie Dentière died in Geneva.

ANALYSIS: *A VERY USEFUL EPISTLE*

The *Epistle* is composed of three parts: the dedicatory cover letter to Marguerite de Navarre, "A Defense of Women," and the epistle proper.

---

46. Diefendorf gives an excellent account of these events and their context in *Beneath the Cross*, esp. 50–56.

47. Kemp proposed that theory of Dentière's role in the 1561 volumes at the Femmes Ecrivains IV conference held in Charlottesville in 1999: "Marie d'Ennetières et la Réforme calviniste: Hypothèses à partir d'une édition de 1561." I thank him for sharing his unpublished research with me.

The Dedicatory Address

The dedicatory address to Marguerite de Navarre begins by asserting women's need to be informed and to inform each other about dangerous evils and the religious doctrines that can guide and protect women against them. It alludes to Calvin and Farel's expulsion from the city and laments the general corruption of the times and the "dissensions and divisions" that reign in all levels of society, from families to nations. Dentière asks Marguerite to implore her brother, Francis I, to intervene. She insists on the right of women to interpret and teach the Bible and addresses her letter also to "other women held in captivity" and "poor little women desiring to know and understand the truth." The Mazarine copy refers to the little Hebrew grammar that her daughter has written in French for the use of other young girls and which she offers as a gift to Marguerite's young daughter, Jeanne. Dentière deplores the attitude that deprives women access to the Bible and expresses a hope that her letter to Marguerite and Marguerite's subsequent cooperation will help to make women less scorned. In the epistle proper she attacks men of power in both the Catholic and the Reformed Churches, thereby indirectly supporting her argument that women should have a greater voice in the church.

A Defense of Women

The pages comprising "A Defense of Women" belong to the literary tradition of illustrious women, following authors such as Boccaccio and Christine de Pizan. Dentière's "Defense" also contributes to the *querelle des femmes*, a series of works beginning in the late fourteenth century that either defended or excoriated women.[48] In a stirring rebuttal of misogynist discourse, Dentière presents a litany of strong and eloquent women from both the Old and New Testaments. Sarah, Rebecca, the mother of Moses, Deborah, Ruth, the queen of Sheba: Dentière enlists all of them, as well as Mary, Elizabeth, the Samaritan woman, and Mary Magdalene, in order to make her case. She attacks the notion that women are the source of evil and insists that they are capable of interpreting Scripture and entitled to do so and to teach one another. She calls on biblical authority to defend women's right to a public voice in religious matters. She counters Paul's injunction *tacient mulieres* (let the women be silent) by evoking the gospels of John and Mark, in which Jesus, to reveal his resurrection, first sent an angel to women and then told a woman, Mary

48. See the series editors' introduction in this volume (xix–xxi). Jordan, in *Renaissance Feminism*, examines defenses of women as well as the misogynistic works to which they respond.

Magdalene, to spread the news to the apostles. Dentière uses the words preach (*prescher*) and female preacher (*prescheresse*) in the "Defense," conveying her conviction that women should not simply teach doctrine to other women in private but should preach to both men and women, "openly before everyone."

Dentière's "Defense" echoes in several places Henricus Cornelius Agrippa's *Declamation on the Nobility and Preeminence of the Female Sex*, which was composed in 1509 and circulated in manuscript before being published in Antwerp in 1529. Originally published in Latin, it was translated into French soon thereafter.[49] Where Agrippa stresses the beauty of the women he names, Dentière stresses their virtue.

The Epistle Proper

While continuing its attacks on a variety of adversaries, the epistle itself presents at length Dentière's convictions on some of the most sharply debated theological questions of the Reformation.[50] For Dentière, the sole authority and source of Christian doctrine is the Bible, especially the New Testament. She affirms that faith in Christ alone is the Christian's means of salvation and reconciliation with God, and decries "false prophets" who have tried to replace him. She implies that the clergy of the Catholic Church are like the Scribes and Pharisees of the Gospels who presumed to be more important than Jesus and his Apostles. Her vision is often apocalyptic, evoking the conflicts and disasters that will announce the return of Christ to earth, the end of the world, and the Last Judgment. She imagines a speech made by Christ to his followers, encouraging them to expect violent persecution as the necessary fulfillment of prophecy that will precede his second coming. She warns against more false prophets to come.

Dentière denounces as slavish external rituals and idolatries pious prac-

49. Agrippa, *Declamation on the Nobility and Preeminence of the Female Sex*. For the diffusion of Agrippa's work and its influence, see in particular, 27–29 and 39, n. 3. From 1524 to 1526, Agrippa was the personal physician of Louise of Savoy, mother of King Francis I and Marguerite de Navarre. Marie Dentière may have heard of him through Marguerite even before his *Declamation* was published. Backus compares Agrippa's and Dentière's praise of women in "Marie Dentière," 184–87.

50. Skenazi situates Dentière in both a theological and a misogynist context in "Marie Dentière et la prédication des femmes," and Backus examines the doctrinal issues raised in the *Epistle* in "Marie Dentière: Un cas de féminisme théologique à l'époque de la Réforme?" In a paper delivered in Sherbrooke in June 1998, "La vision théologique de Marie d'Ennetières," Denommé analyzes Dentière's theology and language, stressing the *Epistle's* similarities with the texts of the Neuchâtel reformers active between 1530 and 1540. She concludes that Froment and Dentière collaborated on the *Epistle*.

tices identified with the Roman Catholic Church, such as pilgrimages and the veneration of saints. She objects to celibacy for priests and to the prohibition against eating meat on certain days. Those objections are part of a much larger debate in Church history about the role that people can play in their own salvation. The *Epistle* affirms the evangelical position upheld by Lefèvre and later by Farel and Calvin that rituals are vain efforts because individuals cannot merit salvation through external actions or "good works." Only through an interior disposition of the soul, through faith, can people be saved. Dentière summarizes that position succinctly:

> Therefore in these times we must not look to ceremonies, sacrifices or visible signs, expecting salvation by exterior and visible things that are administered by men. For if it is the case that man is not justified by works, by the law, nor even by observing all that God commands, but solely by the mercy of God, having faith in his son Jesus, how then will we expect salvation by means of those things which are directly made and ordained by men against God and his word? And therefore we must stop and hold on exclusively to interior goods, to faith, to the spirit opening through charity in our hearts, no matter what the wise proclaim. (64)

The primacy of faith and the inefficacy of works were beliefs shared by Lutherans and the French evangelicals, and they continued to be central doctrines in the Reformed Church of Geneva.[51]

Dentière attacks in particular the Catholic mass, which she describes as a levitic sacrifice that turns "the poor people into idolators who adore the bread and wine as their own God." The Eucharist, the sacrament of the body and blood of Christ, was a central point of disagreement between the reformers and the Catholic Church. The Catholic doctrine of transubstantiation asserted the "real presence" of Christ in the Eucharist; it declared that the priest, with the words of consecration in the Mass, *hoc est enim corpus meum* and *hic est enim calix sanguinis mei* (this is my body, this is the chalice of my blood), changed bread and wine into the body and blood of Christ. While Lutherans and the Anglican Church retained belief in the real presence of Christ in the Eucharist, many reformers saw the bread and wine of communion instead as a sign or symbol commemorating the Last Supper and Christ's death in the crucifixion. Marie Dentière uses the words *sign* and *signify* to describe the way bread and wine represent the body and blood of Christ. She

---

51. The development of those beliefs among the early French reformers is traced by Hughes in *Lefèvre: Pioneer of Ecclesiastical Renewal in France*, 69–100.

calls the Catholic Church doctrine an idolatry that makes the faithful adore the bread and wine.

The *Epistle's* attack on the mass should be understood in the context of earlier works against the mass by Farel, Viret, and especially Marcourt—works that Dentière would have known well from her early association with Farel and from the contacts she and her husband would have had with the Neuchâtel supporters of the Geneva Reformation. The *Epistle* recapitulates the four articles of Marcourt's 1534 placards: Jesus' sacrifice was perfect and cannot be repeated; Jesus is not present in the bread and wine of the mass; claiming that the priest changes the bread and wine into the body and blood of Christ (the doctrine of transubstantiation) is arrogant and presumptuous; and unlike the ritual of the mass, the Reformed communion service of the Lord's Supper leads to a simple, public declaration of faith in salvation through Christ.[52]

Dentière also rejects the Catholic sacrament of Penance and the essential role it gave to the priest in absolving sins. She insists that only God can forgive sins and that Jesus is the only mediator in the reconciliation between God and sinners. Private auricular confession of one's sins to a priest was a relatively recent development in the Catholic Church. It originated in certain monastic orders and was codified only in 1216 by the Fourth Lateran Council, which decreed that all Catholics had to confess their sins to a priest at least once a year. That decree made the priest's absolution of the penitent's sins a necessary requirement and, in effect, gave the priest ecclesiastically validated authority over the penitent's access to forgiveness and justification. Most Reformation leaders disagreed with that position and argued that con-

---

52. For the controversy about the nature of the Eucharist, see the articles by that name in *A Catholic Dictionary of Theology* and the *Oxford Encyclopedia of the Reformation*. For a more detailed study, see Elwood, *The Body Broken*. For the earlier works on the mass written by Dentière's associates in the Reform movement, see Higman, *Lire et découvrir*, 233–88 ("Les débuts de la polémique contre la messe"); see also Farel's 1534 *Sommaire et brève déclaration*, which contains a section on the mass, in his *Le sommaire de G. Farel*, section 19; and the text of the placards in Higman, *La diffusion de la Réforme en France, 1520–1565*, 72–75. Calvin's 1541 *Petit traicté de la saincte Cene de Nostre Seigneur Jesus Christ* is included in Calvin, *Three French Treatises*, 99–130. Marguerite de Navarre does not seem to have shared with those writers a general antipathy for the mass. In each of the eight prologues in the *Heptameron*, group attendance at mass follows the morning scriptural reading led by Oisille. The scriptural readings are the high point of the morning, but the mass is nonetheless a positive setting for contemplating the Holy Spirit. On day three the storytellers contemplate Oisille's lesson with such happiness that they fail to hear the church bell calling them to mass, and they must be summoned by one of the monks. On day four Oisille proposes that the mass be a "penance" where "[we] ask Our Lord to give us the will and the means to obey his commandments." They hear that mass "devoutly." On day seven the group hears "with great devotion" the Mass of the Holy Spirit.

trition, repentance, and forgiveness were effected between the Christian and God alone.[53]

Dentière is scathing in her attack on the venality and corruption of the clergy. She sees greed as the motive behind many pious practices encouraged by the priests: devotion to saints, veneration of images such as the crucifix, tithing, indulgences, and pardons. The clergy are portrayed as rapacious, preying on the vulnerabilities of the poor and the ignorant. She suggests that Catholic persecution of dissident groups is motivated as much by a desire to seize their property as by the will to suppress heretics.[54]

The *Epistle's* attack on the papacy and the worldly structure of the Roman Catholic Church shows Dentière's familiarity with the administrative and legal institutions of the Church that have, in her view, distanced it from the church described in the Gospels and Epistles. Her education about those institutions may have had its foundation while she was still a nun in the Augustinian convent of Tournai, and her criticisms of them would have grown through her experience with the reformed communities of Strasbourg and in the struggles to establish the Reformed Church in Switzerland. She refers to canon law, the body of ecclesiastical legislation as accumulated over the centuries in bishops' letters and especially papal letters called *decretals*. She names the decretals as members of the church hierarchy would have known them, by abbreviated versions of their Latin titles, a string of syllables that would sound like nonsense to the uninitiated. At one point she clusters a group of those titles and a rapid summary of their contents in a staccato style that ridicules the decretals.[55]

In the dedicatory letter, Dentière had asked Marguerite de Navarre to urge her brother the king to intervene, but she had given no details about the kind of action she wanted from Francis. In the epistle proper she becomes

53. Tentler's *Sin and Confession on the Eve of the Reformation* gives an excellent history of the evolving Catholic doctrine of penance and the reformers' criticisms of it. In her *Heptameron* Marguerite de Navarre dramatized the abuses many reformers saw in the Catholic doctrine and practice of confession. See McKinley, "Telling Secrets." Droz offers four works that provide good background for the early Reformation polemic about confession in *Chemins de l'hérésie*, 1–88.

54. Criticism of the clergy's greed and attachment to worldly goods can be found for centuries before the Protestant Reformation. Movements to reform religious orders from within occurred regularly in the later Middle Ages. Erasmus attacked the materialism of monks in many of his writings, for example, in *The Praise of Folly*. Marcourt published a virulent and very popular satire of the clergy's greed, portraying them as merchants in *Le Livre des Marchans* or *Book of Merchants* (1533). There is no modern edition of that work, but Berthoud quotes representative passages from it in *Antoine Marcourt*, 111–56. Dentière's image of the money-hungry clergy joins that tradition.

55. Irena Backus has analyzed some of Dentière's references to canon law, concluding that she knew the decretals well and manipulated them to her own purpose of discrediting canon law.

bolder and more specific, both demanding and accusing. She names neither Francis nor his sister, but when she invokes the honor and power of "God, kings, princes and lords" in an epistle addressed to Marguerite, there can be no doubt about which royal powers she is targeting: "[A]llow the truth to be preached in your lands and kingdoms, so that you and your poor people be led no longer by those miserable blind men." By implication, Francis is one of the blind being led by those blind men, whom Dentière identifies as the powerful French cardinals and bishops at the royal court. They were seen by Marie Dentière and the Swiss reformers as "miserable blind men" who led Francis and prevented the "truth" from being preached in France. "Will you put up with them and let them dominate you?" she asks.

However, the conservative defenders of Catholic orthodoxy are not Dentière's only targets in the *Epistle*. She addresses her complaint directly to Marguerite and implicates members of the clergy who had worked for evangelical reform and whom Marguerite favored. Even though she continued to protect evangelical reformers and to write poetry that expressed their common beliefs, Marguerite de Navarre and some members of her circle were strongly criticized by the Swiss reformers for not following their example and breaking openly with the Catholic Church. They were particularly incensed by Gérard Roussel, Marguerite's chaplain. With Guillaume Farel, Roussel had been a student of Lefèvre d'Etaples and had left Meaux and gone to Strasbourg with Lefèvre in 1525, while Farel was also there. Later, Roussel had, at Marguerite's invitation, preached a series of Lenten sermons at the Louvre in 1533, evangelical sermons that had enraged the Faculty of Theology. Marguerite had protected Roussel from them. However, Roussel never broke with the Catholic Church as Farel had done. In 1536 he was named bishop of Oloron in southwest France, a bishopric that Marguerite obtained for him within the safer realm of her husband, Henry of Navarre. In 1537 Calvin wrote a letter strongly castigating Roussel for compromising his beliefs by accepting a position in the Church he had criticized. In 1544 he would publish his treatise *Against the Nicodemites* giving that caustic nickname to those who, in his opinion, compromised and dissembled their reformist convictions, staying within the Catholic Church to avoid persecution. Marie Dentière's *Epistle* shows that she was well aware of Roussel's appointment and Calvin's reaction to it, a reaction she shared. The French reformers expressed greater contempt for their former comrades than they did for the Catholic hierarchy who had always opposed them. Dentière saves for near the end of her message her most scathing appraisal of one of those men, Pierre Caroli.

In her conclusion Dentière returns to her attack on the councillors of Geneva and on the ministers who replaced the exiled Calvin and Farel. By associating those men with the hated leaders of the Catholic Church and with the recreant Nicodemites, she shows the depth of her contempt for them. She accuses them of venal cowardice, portraying them as men driven by base self-interest rather than by the courage of their convictions, and calling them "cowardly soldiers in battle, . . . bold as slugs." The *Epistle* closes with a biblical allusion that introduces the word *froment* (wheat) as a coded signature, a punning allusion to Antoine Froment and his collaboration in the project.[56] A final reference to Apocalypse (or the Book of Revelation) chapter 18 portrays the Catholic Church as the great Babylon.

PREFACE TO CALVIN'S SERMON

The biblical passage that Calvin treats in his sermon, 1 Timothy 2:8–12, is one of the Pauline passages traditionally quoted to authorize rules of modest dress and appearance for women. In the context of its surrounding verses, it is also one of the principal passages invoked to authorize the silencing of women in public. Paul writes:

> I will therefore that men pray in every place, lifting up pure hands, without anger and contention. In like manner, women also in decent apparel: adorning themselves with modesty and sobriety, not with plaited hair, or gold, or pearls, or costly attire: But, as it becometh women professing godliness, with good works. Let the women learn in silence with all subjection. But I suffer not a woman to teach, nor to use authority over the man: but to be in silence.

Verse 11, along with Paul's injunction: "[L]et the women be silent in the churches," in 1 Corinthians, 14:34, had for centuries been used to justify the silencing of women. In her preface, Marie Dentière assumes the paradoxical position of teaching about a biblical passage that expressly forbade her to do so.

Before examining the preface, we ought to review the text it introduces: Calvin's sermon. Calvin attacks lavish styles in clothing, warning that material luxury leads to other, more serious disorders, such as debauchery. The taste for luxury, Calvin argues, is caused by the sins of vanity, pride, and ambition, sins toward which women are particularly inclined. Women, even more than men, need the refuge and instruction of the Gospel:

56. Slipping a proper name into the end of a literary work was a popular practice among medieval and early Renaissance writers. French poets, such as François Villon and Jean Molinet, whose name means "mill," regularly worked their names, like allusive signatures, into their writings, and François Rabelais made an anagram of his name to identify his narrator Alcofribas Nasier.

So it is that women need God as their refuge as much as men do. They
need, therefore, to be instructed in the Gospel, and so God did not
separate men from women when he gave them the doctrine of salvation. . . . And thus we emphasize that women are not exempt from being taught the word of God.[57]

Women should confess their faith by their actions, and one way women can
show their faith through their actions is by dressing soberly and modestly.
That is true, Calvin insists, for men as well as for women. However, Calvin
makes it clear that modesty poses a different challenge to women than it does
to men:

When St. Paul speaks here of women, he obliges men more than
women to declare their faith. For if anyone were to be excused, it is certain that it would be women more than men—because of their infir-
mity. And so we must give support to these poor, fragile creatures.

Women, in particular, are too inclined to vanity, what Calvin calls "that desire to adorn themselves in order to be looked at from afar." Calvin uses very
strong language to describe that female weakness, calling it "that seething
appetite," and insisting that "that cupidity that women have to adorn themselves is like a raging beast." So strong is women's vanity that it has frustrated
men's attempts to regulate dress by law. Calvin laments the fact that unbe-
lieving pagans had more success in the past than the magistrates of his own
time have had in passing and enforcing laws against "such important and excessive sumptuosities."

It was just three years later that Geneva moved to rectify the situation
Calvin decried, passing sumptuary ordinances in October, 1558.[58] Those
laws, forbidding extravagant attire and lavish spending on banquets, were to
remain on the books throughout the sixteenth century and beyond, prevailing much more successfully in Geneva than in any city of France in which
they were passed. Calvin's remarks in his sermon reflect his dismay at the situation the sumptuary ordinances were enacted to correct.

Today women are more out of bounds than ever. Above all if one goes
to the great courts, it's hard to tell the difference between the men and
the women. It's true that the men are just as bad. Men wear women's
clothes and women wear men's—to the point where there is a terrible

57. I translate directly from the 1561 volume. Calvin's sermon in the original French may be
found in *Ioannis Calvini opera quae supersunt omniae*, vol. 54 in *Corpus Reformatorum*, col. 197–210.

58. See Gallatin, "Les Ordonnances somptuaires à Genève au XVIᵉ siècle"; and Hunt, *Governance
of the Consuming Passions*.

confusion, as if the world had conspired to turn the order of nature up-
side down. It is like signs on taverns, except that the door is open to all
drinkers. So it is that women who dress up like that to attract the eyes
and the glance of men seem to be laying their snares. It's as if they were
making a public tavern of their bodies."

The passage is striking not only for its suggestion of gender confusion in the
courtly fashions of the time, but also for its reference to taverns as a metaphor
for women's transgression into the domain of the masculine. It is all the more
interesting because the taverns—and indeed the whole question of gender-
specific dressing evoked here—call to mind the letter Calvin wrote to Farel
about his hostile encounter with Dentière in 1546, when "in all the taverns,
she began to harangue against long garments."

At the end of his remarks on women's modesty in clothing, Calvin goes
on to comment on the last verse of the passage from 1 Timothy 2:11: "After
St. Paul spoke of women's adornment, he adds that they must learn in silence
and repose, with all subjection. He says this because there are many women
who try to be wiser and who have greater desire for self-promotion than do
men. We see, I say, that mad ambition, and that is to battle against God and
nature." Here again, Calvin attenuates the injunction on women, or at least
expands it, by applying it also to men: "It is true that in general men must
learn this lesson, just as women must. So it is not just for women that they
may learn: men must also apply it to themselves." Calvin admonishes all
those who would teach to remain humble, not to presume they possess wisdom, but to recognize their inherent ignorance: "Because our true wisdom is
to know we are ignorant, in order always to be more and more confirmed in
good doctrine. And thus we do not think that this be different between men
and women, that women must learn, that no one must feel exempt from this
law."

Marie Dentière's preface opens with an extended military metaphor. She
portrays the vigilant Christian (she uses the pronoun *we*) defending a fortress
against the invasion of Satan, paying particular attention to the vulnerable
places where Satan might gain a foothold. By analogy, the ministers of the
church must be alert to identify the vices that threaten their people and work
to extirpate them. John Calvin is just such a minister, but so in a sense, by her
printed preface, is Marie Dentière. She introduces Calvin's sermon on Paul
and thereby appropriates to some extent the role of teacher and minister of
God's word. She succeeds in delivering through print what opposition to
women preachers prevented her from delivering in the pulpit. Her preface
becomes a shorter sermon in its own right. She reinforces Calvin's message

about women's modesty in clothing, but she adds an additional lesson, a diatribe against women who use cosmetics, calling makeup the "work of the devil." In his sermon, Calvin had barely mentioned that topic, referring to makeup only once and in passing. The evil of makeup is, however, a prominent issue in the text of St. Cyprian that follows Calvin's sermon in the two editions containing the preface. That aspect of women's extravagant apparel becomes an important target of Dentière's invective in her preface.

In her remarks on dress and apparel, Dentière seconds Calvin's attack on immodesty and extravagance, but she presents those vices as primarily feminine failings. The concession that men, too, can be guilty of them is far less explicit than in the sermon. Dentière introduces an additional aspect of the argument, one based on wealth, and in that regard both men and women are specified. The overall moral lesson of the preface is that too much concern with adornment of the body threatens to distract the Christian from preserving the well-being of the soul, a caution addressed to men and women alike. Compared to Dentière's *Epistle,* the preface to Calvin's sermon appears less feminist in its outlook. Where the 1539 *Epistle,* with its eloquent "A Defense of Women," argued for the moral equality of men and women and emphasized women's virtues, the 1561 preface to Calvin's sermon conveys a more guarded view: "As for women, who are in that regard [desiring beautiful clothing] more covetous than men, may they understand that too much daring has always been associated with immodesty; likewise, on the contrary, simplicity in clothes has always been a mark of chastity and countenance." However, if an important motivation for the preface was to counter Catholic assertions that Calvinist men and women were given to loose morals, that more cautious view of women may reflect the rhetorical savvy of its author, as well as her acute awareness of the social and political realities facing women as persecution became more intense. The vigilant Christian defending her fortress had more than Satan to fear.

Dentière's preface also reflects the tradition of pedagogical treatises and conduct manuals that were very widely read in the sixteenth century, many of which advocated education for women. Juan Luis Vives's *On the Education of a Christian Woman,* published in 1524, enjoyed enormous popularity, in both its original Latin and its many translations. Chapter 8 of Book 1 in that work "On Adornment" opens with a reference to the same verses from Paul's Epistle to Timothy that inspired Calvin's sermon.[59] Vives attacks what he calls the "insanities" of cosmetics, and he quotes the same St. Cyprian whose admonitions follow Calvin's sermon. Like Dentière, Vives associates modest

59. See Vives, *On the Education of a Christian Woman,* 94–109.

adornment with chastity: "Those women are accounted more beautiful in whom a modest and respectable adornment commends their good character" and "Who could describe what a loss of chastity results from this competition in adornment?"[60] Dentière refers briefly to "the mother of the Gracchi," Cornelia, whom Vives praises frequently as an exemplary model of virtue.

MARIE DENTIÈRE'S POSTERITY

In the years following her death, Marie Dentière all but disappeared from memory. La Croix du Maine, in his 1584 *Bibliothèque Française* referred to her as the author of the *Epistle*, as did Valère André in 1643, calling her a *mulier docta*, or learned woman. In the late nineteenth century, Swiss scholar Aimé-Louis Herminjard published a monumental collection of more than 1,430 letters written by and to the French reformers. His *Correspondance*, an extremely valuable documentary history of the reform movement in French-speaking countries, remains a standard tool for students of the Reformation. In volume five, Herminjard includes an excerpt from Marie Dentière's *Epistle*.[61] In his initial footnote commenting on the *Epistle*, Herminjard calls it "this rarest of works." Indeed, the Geneva volume he used was for many years thought to be the only extant copy. Herminjard includes the dedicatory letter to Marguerite de Navarre and selections from the body of the epistle, marking by ellipses places where he cut passages. Although his stated goal for his project was to offer "an exact as possible reproduction of the texts" (1: xi), he omits without noting its absence the "Defense of Women." Herminjard's footnotes show a marked antipathy for Marie Dentière. He introduces her as Froment's wife, "a resolute woman, who had much education and could 'dogmatize' with the aplomb of a preacher" (5: 151, n. 16). His verb *dogmatiser* can mean simply "to teach doctrine." However, in French usage when applied to women, the word generally conveys a deprecating and pejorative connotation, "to meddle in arguing without any authority."[62]

Herminjard's treatment of Marie Dentière and her writing is strikingly similar to that of the Geneva pastors who suppressed her work, and his com-

---

60. Ibid., 99 and 103.

61. Herminjard, *Correspondance*, 5: 295–304 (no. 785).

62. Littré, *Dictionnaire de la langue française* (Paris: Hachette, 1877): "Se mêler de raisonner là où rien ne nous y authorise. C'était principalement des femmes qui dogmatisaient sous le voile de la sainteté, BOSS[uet]. *Etats d'orais.* I,11. Si vous saviez comme elle dogmatise sur la religion, SEV[igné]. 36. (2: 1206)" [To meddle in arguing where nothing authorizes you to do so. It was principally women who dogmatized under the veil of sanctity. . . . If you knew how she dogmatizes about religion].

ments about her echo misogynistic attitudes common in sixteenth-century Europe, attitudes that she attacks in her *Epistle*. His manner of representing Dentière recalls the church leaders, her adversaries, who refused women access to the ministry. Herminjard, unlike Beatus Comte, allows that Dentière was the author of the letter. However, he undermines her role in other ways. In the final note to the *Epistle*, he raises the question of the authorship of the work, entertaining and then dismissing the possibility that it was Froment who wrote it:

> Must we conclude that the Dauphinois Reformer was the real author of the *Epistle?* We do not think so. He could have given his wife the ideas, the arguments, some nice turns of phrase, and the Latin quotations from the canons and the decretals that are in the passages that we have suppressed. His collaboration must have been limited to that. (5: 304, n. 23)

Herminjard was refuting assumptions expressed in contemporary documents that Froment was the author of the *Epistle*.[63] However, his concession that Froment might have furnished his wife with the ideas, arguments, quotations from Latin sources and phrasing—in effect, the substance of the letter—leaves very little credit due to Marie Dentière. Although Herminjard goes on to compliment Marie Dentière's style, he has already undermined the compliment: "The style seems to us far superior to Froment's: it is livelier, more alert, more direct and never betrays the slightest hesitation of the writer" (5: 304,n. 23). His praise of her style after refusing her credit for the ideas and erudition of the work reinforces a notion that women may have access to public voice in an aesthetic register, as poets or authors of fiction perhaps, but not as serious intellectuals and political agents, not as creators and promulgators of ideas that could redistribute power.

In the other volumes of his *Correspondance*, Herminjard is even more hostile to Marie Dentière. In his comments on the letter in which the ministers of Berne complain of Froment's double career as a merchant and a pastor, he writes,

> This proud and vindictive woman was, in spite of her intelligence, a bad counselor for her new husband, whom she dominated absolutely.

---

63. Herminjard's *Correspondance* includes two letters written by the Council of Berne, one to the Council of Geneva on May 23, 1539 (5: 321–22 [no. 792]) and another to Pierre Viret and Beatus Comte on June 14, 1539 which refer to "Froment's book" (5: 332–33 [no. 796]). The resumé of Beatus Comte's report to the Council of Berne refers to "Froment's little book" (5: 332–33, nn. 2–3).

She prepared his moral downfall, by allowing him to seek in business a life of ease that his pastoral career could not give him. And thus, during the whole week, he ran a grocery shop, and on Sundays he climbed into the pulpit. When he was transferred to Thonon (1537), Froment speculated heavily in wine, in oil, and, ever greedier, he added to his duties as deacon those of tollkeeper. Business worthy of a real Demas, said the pastors of Chablais in a letter that we will give farther on.[64]

Herminjard, blaming the failings of Froment on his wife, is much harsher in his judgment than Calvin eventually was. This view of the evil influence of the wife on her husband continues in a later note where Herminjard records Froment's trip to Lyon to speak to Francis and Marguerite:

Francis I, who was on July 29 and again on August 2 in Argilly, near Beaune, and on the 8th in Trévoux, made his entry into Lyon on the 9th. His sister, Marguerite, queen of Navarre, accompanied him. This trip of the court must have keenly interested Marie Dentière, Froment's wife, who had earlier friendly relations with the queen of Navarre, and had even addressed her *Very Useful Epistle* to her. This ambitious and scheming woman made her husband go to Lyon, so that they could pay their respects to the sister of the King.[65]

Herminjard's attribution of Froment's moral downfall to his wife recalls Farel's 1538 letter and perpetuates a well-established misogynist tradition that flourished in Dentière's time, the notion that women are responsible for men's failings. Advocates of that notion used the Genesis story of the Fall to support their position. Simontault, the narrator of the first tale in Marguerite de Navarre's *Heptameron*, is one of them: "Just consider now, Ladies, the amount of trouble that was caused by one woman. . . . I think you'll agree that ever since Eve made Adam sin, women have taken it upon themselves to torture men, kill them and damn them to Hell."[66] Whether or not Eve was responsible for Adam's fall generated theological debate among the early church fathers and continued to preoccupy the reformers. Women's inherited guilt and additional responsibility for subsequent sins of men was an issue central to that debate.[67]

64. Ibid., 6: 173–74, n. 28. See 6: 401–4 (no. 927) for the later letter.
65. Ibid., 8: 106, n. 14–15.
66. Marguerite de Navarre, *Heptameron*, 78.
67. For the misogynist tradition tracing evil back to Eve and a sin that she made Adam commit, see McLaughlin, "Equality of Souls, Inequality of Sexes"; Warner, *Alone of All Her Sex: The Myth and the Cult of the Virgin Mary*, 50–67; Miles, *Carnal Knowing: Female Nakedness and Religious Meaning in the*

On what evidence did Herminjard base his harsh judgment of Marie Dentière? Do the sixteenth-century documents he knew justify the portrait of her as a proud, vindictive, ambitious, scheming, resolute woman with pretensions to the pulpit, who was a bad influence on her husband, bringing about his moral ruin because she urged him to run a grocery business during the week? And are the judgments expressed in contemporary documents based on anything besides preconceived attitudes toward women that are themselves misogynous? The letters in Herminjard's *Correspondance* and other documents from Dentière's time make it clear that she often rankled her contemporaries. She persisted in forcefully expressing her convictions without caring about others' reactions; she used colorful, even crude, language to voice her anger; and she was an outspoken activist, even an extremist, in the struggles of the Reformation. However, the same could be said of many of her contemporaries, men whom Herminjard presents without criticism.

NOTE ON THE TRANSLATIONS: MARIE DENTIÈRE'S LANGUAGE AND RHETORIC

Marie Dentière writes with an energy and rhythm that often suggest oral delivery. Her style recalls that of her early colleagues Farel, Viret, and Marcourt, for example, and it gives us an idea of how she might have addressed a congregation if she had been allowed access to the pulpit. Her works composed for publication show familiarity with the rhetorical techniques of an effective sermon. The identity of the second-person "you" to whom Dentière speaks shifts without warning within the *Epistle*, as does that of the first-person "I." At times, the speaking "I" is the voice of Jesus Christ addressing his faithful. Usually, the "you" suggests a general audience, the "all without exception" whom she designates in the opening line of the epistle proper, a group who could be sitting in the pews listening to a preacher. However, she shifts abruptly into scathing accusations addressed with equal vigor to the prelates of the Catholic Church and to the councillors of Geneva. Later, showing little restraint or deference, she targets royal authorities, chastising them for their cowardice and inaction, including by implication Marguerite de Navarre. Such changes of her implied audience, accompanied by an appropriate tone of voice, would heighten the dramatic quality of a sermon.

Dentière's sentences are often very long, and at times they show little re-

---

Christian West, 85–116; and Bloch, *Medieval Misogyny and the Invention of Western Romantic Love*, 65–91. For a thorough treatment of Calvinist interpretations of Eve and her role in the fall, see Thompson, *John Calvin and the Daughters of Sarah*, 107–59. For a sample of Renaissance representations of Eve in prints, see Russell, *Eva/Ave: Women in Renaissance and Baroque Prints*, 113–29.

gard for syntax. She often begins a sentence with a conjunction, usually "and" or "but." The rhythmic qualities of her language also suggest that oral delivery was never far from her mind as she wrote for publication. She emphasizes a point with a string of examples, the length of which can jar the expectations of a modern reader. She is fond of words and phrases in groups of twos and especially threes, a repetition that would have helped an audience to absorb the speaker's message. Shifts from one topic to another occur with little warning, and her tone can become suddenly ironic. In those cases we can imagine that a pause or change in tone in oral delivery would compensate for the lack of transitions. Quotations, paraphrases, and cadences from the Bible are frequent in the *Epistle,* and the Bible supplies many of its colorful metaphors. Several passages are simply a succession of biblical quotations. References printed in the margins of the text, included in this translation, identified many of those biblical sources or pointed to other scriptural passages. A few of those marginal notations are out of order or seem irrelevant to the passages they accompany. Polemical works like the *Epistle,* especially when they were printed clandestinely, may bear the traces of their hasty production. I have corrected a few obvious errors in the biblical references, but I have left the rest as they appear in the margins. Along with the biblical references, the text and margins contain references to canon law, the body of rules or laws that accumulated gradually over the centuries to govern the Catholic Church. One marginal reference may point to a scandal involving Dominican clerics that occurred thirty years earlier in Berne.

The *Epistle* bears no page numbers. It does have signatures, letters and numbers on the bottom of most pages that help the printer to fold the printed sheets into sets of leaves, called "gatherings" or "quires," and to place them in the proper sequence. The *Epistle* has four gatherings, lettered *a, b, c,* and *d,* making a total of thirty-two leaves, or sixty-four unnumbered pages. There are eight leaves per gathering, a1 to a8, for example. The right-hand page, or front side (recto), of the first leaf is a1r or simply a, and the reverse side (verso) of that leaf is a1v. I have used the signature notations to indicate, in brackets, where each new page begins, starting with the dedicatory address on a2r. In the volume I consulted at the Bibliothèque municipale in Lunel, the preface to Calvin's sermon begins on b4r and ends on b6v.[68]

My translation attempts to make Dentière's language more accessible to the modern reader without losing the characteristic rhythm and flavor of her style. I have broken some very long sentences into shorter ones, and I have

---

68. For more about the early modern printed book and its parts, see McKerrow, *An Introduction to Bibliography for Literary Students.*

smoothed some awkward syntax, but I have retained her series of examples and tried to convey the cadence of her prose. As usual in printed works from this period, neither the original *Epistle* nor the preface to Calvin's sermon contains paragraph breaks. I have made paragraphs in the translation, hoping to show how Dentière develops her ideas as her writing unfolds.

VOLUME EDITOR'S
BIBLIOGRAPHY

PRIMARY SOURCES

Agrippa, Henricus Cornelius. *Declamation on the Nobility and Preeminence of the Female Sex.* Trans. and ed. Albert Rabil Jr. The Other Voice in Early Modern Europe. Chicago: University of Chicago Press, 1996.

Bonivard, François. *Chroniques de Genève.* Vol. 1. Ed. Micheline Tripet. Textes Littéraires Français. Geneva: Droz, 2001.

Bossard, Maurice, and Louis Junod, eds. *Chroniqueurs du XVIe siècle: Bonivard, Pierrefleur, Jeanne de Jussie, Fromment.* Lausanne: Bibliothèque romande, 1974.

Calvin, John. *Ioannis Calvini opera quae supersunt omnia.* 59 vols. Ed. G. Baum, E. Cunitz, and E. Reuss. Vols. 29–87 of *Corpus Reformatorum.* Brunswick and Berlin: Schwetschke, 1863–1900. Reprint, New York: Johnson Reprints, 1964.

———. *Letters of John Calvin.* Ed. Jules Bonnet. 2 vols. 1858. Reprint, New York: Lenox Hill (Burt Franklin), 1972.

———. *Three French Treatises.* Ed. Francis Higman. London: Athlone Press, 1970.

———. *Treatises against the Anabaptists and against the Libertines.* Trans. and ed. Benjamin W. Farley. Grand Rapids, MI: Baker Book House, 1982.

Dentière, Marie. *Epistre tres utile faicte et composée par une femme Chrestienne de Tornay, Envoyée à la Royne de Navarre seur du Roy de France, Contre Les Turcz, Iuifz, Infideles, Faulx chrestiens, Anabaptistes, et Lutheriens,* [*à Anvers, chez Martin l'empereur*]. Geneva: Jean Gérard, 1539.

———. "Preface to a Sermon by John Calvin." Printed in *Les Conditions et vertus requises en la femme fidèle et bonne mesnagere: Contenues au xxxi. Chapitre des Prouerbes de Salomon. Mis en forme de Cantique, par Théodore de Besze. Plus, un Sermon de la modestie des Femmes en leurs habillemens, par. M. Iean Calvin. Outre, plusieurs chansons spirituelles, en Musique.* 1561.

Erasmus. *Colloquies.* Trans. and ed., Craig R. Thompson. Vol. 40 of *Collected Works of Erasmus.* Toronto: University of Toronto Press, 1997.

Farel, Guillaume. *Le Pater Noster et le Credo en françoys.* Extracts in *La diffusion de la Réforme en France, 1520–1565,* ed. Francis Higman, 27–31. Publications de la Faculté de Théologie de l'Université de Genève, no. 17. Geneva: Editions Labor et Fides, 1992.

———. *Le sommaire de G. Farel, réimprimé d'après l'édition de l'an 1534.* Ed. J.-G. Baum. Geneva: Jules-Guillaume Fick, 1867.

Fromment, Anthoine. *Les actes et gestes merveilleux de la cité de Genève. Nouvellement convertie à l'Evangile faictz du temps de leur Reformation et comment ils l'ont receue redigez par escript en fourme de Chroniques Annales ou Hystoyres commençant l'an MD XXX II*. Ed. Gustave Revilliod. Geneva: Jules-Guillaume Fick, 1854.

La guerre et deslivrance de la ville de Genesve [composée et publiée en 1536 par Marie Dentière de Tournay, ancienne abbesse et femme d'Antoine Froment]. Réimprimée pour la première fois conformément au texte original, avec une introduction et des notes, par Albert Rilliet. Tiré du tome XX des *Mémoires de la Société d'Histoire et d'Archéologie de Genève*. Genève: Imprimerie Charles Schuchardt, 1881. Original title: *La guerre et délivrance de la ville de Genesve fidèlement faicte et composée par un Marchand demourant en icelle* [The war and deliverance of the city of Geneva, faithfully told and written by a merchant living in that city]. Originally published in 1536.

Herminjard, A.-L., ed. *Correspondance des Réformateurs dans les pays de langue française. Recueillie et publiée avec d'autres lettres relatives à la Réforme et des notes historiques et biographiques.* 9 vols. 1866–97. Reprint, Nieuwkoop: B. De Graaf, 1965.

Jussie, Jeanne de. *Le levain du Calvinisme, ou Commencement de l'heresie de Geneve*. Ed. Ad.-C. Grivel. Geneva: Jules-Guillaume Fick, 1865.

———. *Petite chronique*. Einleitung, Edition, Kommentar, von Helmut Feld. Mainz: Verlag Philipp von Zabern, 1996.

Labé, Louise. *Louise Labé: Oeuvres complètes*. Ed. François Rigolot. Paris:Garnier/Flammarion, 1986.

[Marcourt, Antoine]. *Articles veritables sur les horribles, grandz, et importables abuz de la Messe papale: inventée directement contre la saincte Cene de Jesus Christ.* [Neuchâtel: Pierre de Vingle, 1534]. In *La diffusion de la Réforme en France, 1520–1565*, ed. Francis Higman, 72–75. Publications de la Faculté de Théologie de l'Université de Genève, no. 17. Geneva: Editions Labor et Fides, 1992.

Marguerite de Navarre. *Heptaméron*. Ed. Renja Salminen. Geneva: Droz, 1999.

———. *The Heptameron*. Trans. Paul Chilton. New York: Penguin Books, 1984.

———. *Marguerites de la Marguerite des Princesses* [Pearls of the pearl of princesses]. 1547. Ed. Félix Frank, 1873. Reprint, Geneva: Slatkine, 1970.

———. *Miroir de l'âme pécheresse*. Ed. Renja Salminen. Helsinki: Suomalainen, Tiedeakatemia, 1979.

———. *The Mirror of the Sinful Soul*. A prose translation from the French of a poem by Queen Margaret of Navarre, made in 1544 by the Princess (afterward Queen) Elizabeth, then eleven years of age. Reproduced in facsimile, with portrait, for the Royal Society of Literature of the United Kingdom, and edited, with an introduction and notes, by Percy W. Ames. London: Asher, 1897.

———. *Pater Noster et Petit OEuvre dévot*. Ed. Sabine Lardon. Vol. 1 of *OEuvres complètes*. Ed. Niclole Cazauran. Paris: Honoré Champion, 2001.

Montaigne, Michel de. *The Complete Essays of Montaigne*. Trans. Donald M. Frame. Stanford, CA: Stanford University Press, 1958.

———. *Les Essais de Montaigne*. Ed. Pierre Villey and V.-L. Saulnier. 2 vols. Paris: Presses Universitaires Françaises, 1965, 1978.

More, Thomas. *The Complete Works of St. Thomas More*. New Haven, CT: Yale University Press, 1963–.

Rabelais, François. *Gargantua and Pantagruel*. Trans. J. M. Cohen. New York: Penguin Books, 1955.

———. *Oeuvres complètes*. Ed. Mireille Huchon et al. Paris: Gallimard, Bibliothèque de la Pléiade, 1994.

Vives, Juan Luis. *The Education of a Christian Woman: A Sixteenth-Century Manual.* Ed. and trans. Charles Fantazzi. The Other Voice in Early Modern Europe. Chicago: University of Chicago Press, 2000.

SECONDARY SOURCES

Audisio, Gabriel. *The Waldensians: Dissent, Persecution and Survival, c. 1170–c. 1570.* Cambridge: Cambridge University Press, 1999.

Backus, Irena. "Marie Dentière: Un cas de féminisme théologique à l'époque de la Réforme?" *Bulletin de la Société de l'Histoire du Protestantisme Français* 137 (1991): 177–95.

Bartos, F. M. "Picards et 'Pikarti.'" *Bulletin de la Société de l'Histoire du Protestantisme* 80–81 (1931–32): 465–86, 8–28.

Bietenholz, Peter G., and Thomas B. Deutscher, eds. *Contemporaries of Erasmus: A Biographical Register of the Renaissance and Reformation.* 3 vols. Toronto: University of Toronto Press, 1985.

Berthoud, Gabrielle. *Antoine Marcourt, réformateur et pamphlétaire du "Livre des Marchans" aux Placards de 1534.* Geneva: Droz, 1973.

Blackburn, Wm. M. *William Farel and the Story of the Swiss Reform.* Philadelphia, PA: Presbyterian Board of Publication, 1865.

Blaisdell, Charmarie Jenkins. "The Matrix of Reform: Women in the Lutheran and Calvinist Movements." In *Triumph over Silence: Women in Protestant History,* ed. Richard L. Greaves, 13–44. Contributions to the Study of Religion, no. 15. Westport, CT: Greenwood Press, 1985.

———. "Religion, Gender, and Class: Nuns and Authority in Early Modern France." In *Changing Identities in Early Modern France,* ed. Michael Wolfe, 147–68. Durham, NC: Duke University Press, 1999.

Bloch, R. Howard. *Medieval Misogyny and the Invention of Western Romantic Love.* Chicago: University of Chicago Press, 1991.

Bothe, Catherine M. "Ecriture féminine de la Réformation: Le témoignage de Marie Dentière." *Romance Languages Annual* 5 (1993): 15–19.

Cameron, Euan. *Wadenses: Rejections of Holy Church in Medieval Europe.* Oxford: Blackwell, 2000.

A Catholic Dictionary of Theology. 3 vols. New York: Nelson, 1962.

Certeau, Michel de. *The Possession of Loudun.* Trans. Michael B. Smith. Chicago: University of Chicago Press, 2000.

Chrisman, Miriam U. *Strasbourg and the Reform: A Study in the Process of Change.* New Haven, CT: Yale University Press, 1967.

———. "Women and the Reformation in Strasbourg, 1490–1530." *Archiv für Reformationgeschicte* 63 (1972): 143–68.

Clark, Stuart. *Thinking with Demons: The Idea of Witchcraft in Early Modern Europe.* Oxford: Oxford University Press, 1997.

Cottrell, Robert D. *The Grammar of Silence: A Reading of Marguerite de Navarre's Poetry.* Washington, DC: Catholic University of America Press, 1986.

Cross, F. L., ed. *The Oxford Dictionary of the Christian Church.* 3rd ed. Ed. E. A. Livingstone. Oxford: Oxford University Press, 1997.

Crouzet, Denis. *La Genèse de la Réforme française 1520–1560*. Paris: Société d'Édition d'Enseignement Supérieur, 1996.

Davis, Natalie Zemon. *Society and Culture in Early Modern France*. Stanford, CA: Stanford University Press, 1975.

Denommé, Isabelle C. "La vision théologique de Marie d'Ennetières." *Proceedings of the Canadian Society for Renaissance and Reformation Studies*. Forthcoming.

Diefendorf, Barbara. *Beneath the Cross: Catholics and Huguenots in Sixteenth-Century Paris*. New York: Oxford University Press, 1991.

Douglass, Jane Dempsey. "Marie Dentière's Use of Scripture in Her Theology of History." In *Biblical Hermeneutics in Historical Perspective: Studies in honor of Karlfried Froehlich on his Sixtieth Birthday*, ed. Mark Burrows and Paul Rorem, 227–44. Grand Rapids, MI: Wm. B. Eerdmans, 1991.

———. "Women and the Continental Reformation." In *Religion and Sexism: Images of Women in the Jewish and Christian Traditions*, ed. Rosemary R. Ruether, 292–318. New York: Simon and Schuster, 1974.

———. *Women, Freedom, and Calvin*, Philadelphia, PA: Westminster Press, 1985.

Doyle, Robert. "Women's Ministry, Social Flexibility and the Sixteenth Century." *Reformed Theological Review* 46, no. 1 (1987): 1–9.

Droz, Eugénie. *Chemins de l'hérésie: textes et documents*. Geneva: Slatkine Reprints, 1970.

Dufour, Théophile. *Notice bibliographique sur le Cathéchisme et la Confession de foi de Calvin (1537) et sur les autres livres imprimés à Genève et à Neuchâtel dans les premiers temps de la Réforme (1533–1540)*. 1878. Reprint, Geneva: Slatkine, 1970.

Eire, Carlos. *War against the Idols: The Reformation of Worship from Erasmus to Calvin*. Cambridge: Cambridge University Press, 1986.

Elwood, Christopher. *The Body Broken: The Calvinist Doctrine of the Eucharist and the Symbolization of Power in Sixteenth-Century France*. New York and Oxford: Oxford University Press, 1999.

Farge, James K. "Marguerite de Navarre, Her Circle, and the Censors of Paris." In *International Colloquium Celebrating the Five Hundredth Anniversary of the Birth of Marguerite de Navarre*, ed. Régine Reynolds-Cornell, 15–28. Birmingham, AL: Summa Publications, 1995.

Ferguson, Gary. *Mirroring Belief: Marguerite de Navarre's Devotional Poetry*. Edinburgh: Edinburgh University Press, 1992.

Ferguson, Margaret W., Maureen Quilligan, and Nancy J. Vickers, eds. *Rewriting the Renaissance: The Discourses of Sexual Difference in Early Modern Europe*. Chicago: University of Chicago Press, 1986.

Gallatin, Marie-Lucile. "Les Ordonnances somptuaires à Genève au XVIᵉ siècle." In *Mémoires et documents publiés par la société d'histoire et d'archéologie de Genève* 36 (1938): 191–277.

Green, Lowell. "The Education of Women in the Reformation. *History of Education Quarterly* 19, no. 1 (1979): 93–116.

Guillaume Farel, 1489–1565: Biographie nouvelle écrite d'après les documents originaux par un groupe d'historiens, professeurs et pasteurs de Suisse, de France et d'Italie. 1930. Reprint, Geneva: Slatkine, 1978.

Haag, Eugène, ed. *La France protestante*. 5 vols. 2nd ed. Paris: Librairie Sandoz et Fischbacher, 1877–1888. See the article on Marie Dentière in vol. 5 (1886): 238–49.

Head, Thomas. "A Propagandist for the Reform: Marie Dentière." In *Women Writers of the Renaissance and Reformation*, ed. Katharina M. Wilson, 260–83. Athens: University of Georgia Press, 1987.

———. "The Religion of the *Femmelettes*: Ideals and Experience among Women in Fifteenth- and Sixteenth-Century France." In *That Gentle Strength: Historical Perspectives on Women in Christianity*, ed. Lynda Coon, Katherine Haldane, and Elisabeth Sommer, 149–75. Charlottesville: University Press of Virginia, 1991.

Heller, Henry. "Marguerite de Navarre and the Reformers of Meaux." *Bibliothèque d'Humanisme et Renaissance* 33 (1971): 271–301.

Heyer, Henri. *Guillaume Farel: An Introduction to His Theology*. Trans. Blair Reynolds. Texts and Studies in Religion, no. 54. Lewiston, NY: Edward Mellen Press, 1990.

Higman, Francis. "Calvin and Farel." In *Calvinus sacrae scripturae professor*. Grand Rapids, MI: Wm. B. Eerdmans, 1994, 214–23.

———. *La diffusion de la Réforme en France, 1520–1565*. Publications de la Faculté de Théologie de l'Université de Genève, no. 17. Geneva: Editions Labor et Fides, 1992.

———. *Lire et découvrir: La circulation des idées au temps de la Réforme*. Préface de Jean-François Gilmont. Geneva: Droz, 1998.

———. *Piety and the People: Religious Printing in France, 1511–1551*. St. Andrews Studies in Reformation History. Hants, England: Scolar Press, 1996.

———. *The Style of John Calvin in His French Polemical Treatises*. London: Oxford University Press, 1967.

Hillerbrand, Hans, ed. *The Oxford Encyclopedia of the Reformation*. 4 vols. Oxford: Oxford University Press, 1995.

Hollier, Denis, R. Howard Block, Peter Brooks, Joan DeJean, Barbara Johnson, Philip E. Lewis, Nancy K. Miller, François Rigolot, and Nancy J. Vickers, eds. *A New History of French Literature*. Cambridge, MA: Harvard University Press, 1989.

Hornus, Jean-Michel, and Rodolphe Peter. "*Calviniana rarissima* du Fonds Jean-Louis Médard à la Bibliothèque municipale de Lunel." *Etudes théologiques et religieuses*, 54 (1979): 51–68.

Hughes, Philip Edgcumbe. *Lefèvre: Pioneer of Ecclesiastical Renewal in France*. Grand Rapids, MI: Wm. B. Eerdmans, 1984.

Hunt, Alan. *Governance of the Consuming Passions: A History of Sumptuary Law*. New York: St. Martin's Press, 1996.

Jordan, Constance. *Renaissance Feminism: Literary Texts and Political Models*. Ithaca, NY: Cornell University Press, 1990.

Kemp, William. "L'épigraphe 'Lisez et puis jugez': Le 'libre examen' dans la Réforme française avant 1540." Forthcoming in the proceedings of the Sherbrooke Conference, June 2000.

———. "Marguerite of Navarre, Clément Marot, and the Augereau Editions of the *Miroir de l'âme pécheresse* (Paris, 1533)." *Journal of the Early Book Society* 2 (1999): 113–56.

———, and Diane Desrosiers-Bonin. "Marie d'Ennetières et la petite grammaire hébraïque de sa fille d'après la dédicace de l'*Epistre* à Marguerite de Navarre." *Bibliothèque d'Humanisme et Renaissance* 50, no. 1 (1998): 117–34.

Kingdon, Robert. "Was the Protestant Reformation a Revolution? The Case of Geneva." In *Transition and Revolution: Problems and Issues of European Renaissance and Reformation History*, ed. R. Kingdon, 53–107. Minneapolis, MN: Burgess, 1974.

Knecht, R. J. *Catherine de' Medici*. London: Longman, 1998.

———. *Renaissance Warrior and Patron: The Reign of Francis I*. Cambridge: Cambridge University Press, 1994.

Lazard, Madeleine. "Deux soeurs ennemies, Marie Dentière et Jeanne de Jussie: Nonnes et réformées à Genève." In *Les réformes: Enracinements socio-culturels*, ed. B. Chevalier and C. Sauzat, 233–49. Vingt-cinquième colloque d'études humanistes. Tours, 1982. Paris: La Maisnie, 1985.

Maclean, Ian. *The Renaissance Notion of Woman: A Study in the Fortunes of Scholasticism and Medical Science in European Intellectual Life*. Cambridge: Cambridge University Press, 1980.

McKee, Elsie Anne. *Katharina Schütz Zell*. Vol. 1. *The Life and Thought of a Sixteenth-Century Reformer*. Vol. 2. *The Writings: A Critical Edition*. Leiden: Brill, 1999.

McKerrow, Ronald B. *An Introduction to Bibliography for Literary Students*. Oxford: Clarendon Press, 1928. Reprint, with an introduction by David McKitterick, New Castle, DE: Oak Knoll Press, 1994.

McKinley, Mary B. "The Absent Ellipsis: The Edition and Suppression of Marie Dentière in the Sixteenth and the Nineteenth Century." In *Women Writers of the Ancien Régime: Strategies of Emancipation*, ed. Colette Winn, 85–99. New York: Garland, 1997.

———. "Telling Secrets: Sacramental Confession and Narrative Authority in the *Heptameron*." In *Critical Tales: New Studies of the* Heptameron *and Early Modern Culture*, ed. John D. Lyons and Mary B. McKinley, 146–71. Philadelphia: University of Pennsylvania Press, 1993.

McLaughlin, Eleanor. "Equality of Souls, Inequality of Sexes: Women in Medieval Theology." In *Religion and Sexism: Images of Women in the Jewish and Christian Traditions*, ed. Rosemary Radford Ruether, 213–66. New York: Simon and Schuster, 1974.

Meylan, Henri. "Un grand historien: Aimé-Louis Herminjard (1817–1900)." *Musées de Genève*, 7, no. 66 (1966): 4–5.

———. *Silhouettes du XVIᵉ siècle*. Lausanne: Editions de l'Eglise Nationale Vaudoise, 1943.

Miles, Margaret R. *Carnal Knowing: Female Nakedness and Religious Meaning in the Christian West*. Boston: Beacon Press, 1989. Reprint, New York: Vintage Books, 1991.

Monter, E. William. *Calvin's Geneva*. New York: John Wiley & Sons, 1967.

———. *Witchcraft in France and Switzerland: The Borderlands during the Reformation*. Ithaca, NY: Cornell University Press, 1976.

———. "Women in Calvinist Geneva, 1550–1800." *Signs: Journal of Women in Culture and Society* 6, no. 2 (1980): 189–209.

Moreau, Gérard. *Histoire du Protestantisme à Tournai jusqu'à la veille de la Révolution des Pays-Bas*. Paris: Les Belles Lettres, 1962.

Mustard, Wilfred P., ed. *The Eclogues of Faustus Andrelinus and Ioannes Arnolletus*. Baltimore, MD: Johns Hopkins Press, 1918.

Naef, Henri. *Les origines de la Réforme à Genève*. 2 vols. Travaux d'Humanisme et Renaissance. Geneva: Droz, 1968.

The New Schaff-Herzog Encyclopedia of Religious Knowledge. Grand Rapids, MI: Baker, 1949–50.

Ozment, Stephen. "Calvin and Calvinism." Chapter 11 in *The Age of Reform, 1250–1550: An Intellectual and Religious History of Late Medieval and Reformation Europe*. New Haven, CT: Yale University Press, 1980.

Parker, Patricia. *Literary Fat Ladies: Rhetoric, Gender, and Property.* London and New York: Methuen, 1987.

Persels, Jeffery. "Cooking with the Pope." *Mediaevalia* 22 (1999): 29–53.

Peter, Rodolphe, and Jean-François Gilmont. *Bibliotheca Calviniana.* Vol. 2. *Ecrits théologiques, littéraires et juridiques, 1555–1564.* Geneva: Droz, 1994.

Reid, Jonathan. "King's Sister, Queen of Dissent: Marguerite de Navarre (1492–1549) and Her Evangelical Network." Ph.D. diss., University of Arizona, 2001.

Roelker, Nancy Lyman. "The Appeal of Calvinism to French Noblewomen in the Sixteenth Century." *The Journal of Interdisciplinary History* 2, no. 4 (1972): 391–418.

———. *One King, One Faith: The Parlement of Paris and the Religious Reformations of the Sixteenth Century.* Berkeley and Los Angeles: University of California Press, 1996.

———. "The Role of Noblewomen in the French Reformation." *Archiv für Reformationgeschicte* 63 (1972): 168–94.

Roper, Lyndal. *The Holy Household: Women and Morals in Reformation Augsburg,* Oxford: Clarendon Press, 1989.

Russell, H. Diane. *Eva/Ave: Women in Renaissance and Baroque Prints,* Washington: National Gallery of Art with the Feminist Press at the City University of New York, 1990.

Skenazi, Cynthia. "Les annotations en marge du *Miroir de l'ame pecheresse.*" *Bibliothèque d'Humanisme et Renaissance* 55, no. 2 (1993): 255–70.

———. "Marie Dentière et la prédication des femmes." *Renaissance and Reformation/ Renaissance et Réforme* 21, no. 1 (1997): 5–18.

Sluhovsky, Moshe. "The Devil in the Convent." *American Historical Review* 107, no. 5 (2002): 1379–1411.

Sommers, Paula. *Celestial Ladders: Readings in Marguerite de Navarre's Poetry of Spiritual Ascent.* Geneva: Droz, 1989.

Stallybrass, Peter. "Patriarchal Territories: The Body Enclosed." In *Rewriting the Renaissance: The Discourses of Sexual Difference in Early Modern Europe,* ed. Margaret W. Ferguson, Maureen Quilligan, and Nancy J. Vickers, 123–42. Chicago: University of Chicago Press, 1986.

Taylor, Larissa, ed. *Preachers and People in the Reformations and Early Modern Period.* Leiden: Brill, 2001.

Tentler, Thomas. *Sin and Confession on the Eve of the Reformation.* Princeton, NJ: Princeton University Press, 1977.

Thompson, John Lee. *John Calvin and the Daughters of Sarah: Women in Regular and Exceptional Roles in the Exegesis of Calvin, His Predecessors, and His Contemporaries,* Geneva: Droz, 1992.

Thysell, Carol. *The Pleasures of Discernment: Marguerite de Navarre as Theologian.* Oxford Studies in Historical Theology. London: Oxford University Press, 2000.

Tlustly, Beverly Ann. "Gender and Alcohol Use in Early Modern Augsburg." *Histoire Sociale/ Social History* 27, no. 54 (1994): 241–59.

Warner, Marina. *Alone of All Her Sex: The Myth and the Cult of the Virgin Mary.* New York: Random House, 1976. Reprint, New York: Vintage Books, 1983.

Wengler, Elisabeth M. "Women, Religion, and Reform in Sixteenth-Century Geneva." Ph.D. diss. Dept. of History, Boston College, 1999.

Wiesner, Merry. "Beyond Women and the Family: Towards a Gender Analysis of the Reformation." *Sixteenth Century Journal* 28, no. 3 (1987): 311–21.

———. "Women's Defense of Their Public Role." In *Women in the Middle Ages and Re-*

naissance, ed. Mary Beth Rose, 1–27. Syracuse, NY: Syracuse University Press, 1985.

Williams, Wes. *Pilgrimage and Narrative in the French Renaissance: 'The Undiscovered Country.'* Oxford: Clarendon Press, 1998.

Zagorin, Perez. *Ways of Lying: Dissimulation, Persecution, and Conformity in Early Modern Europe.* Cambridge, MA: Harvard University Press, 1990.

A VERY USEFUL EPISTLE

made and composed by a Christian Woman of Tournai
sent to the Queen of Navarre Sister of the King of France.
Against
The Turks, Jews, Infidels, False Christians,
Anabaptists, and Lutherans

READ AND THEN JUDGE

Newly printed in Antwerp
at the shop of Martin L'Empereur
[Geneva: Jean Girard]
M.V^c.XXXIX

Fear not O Land, but be glad and rejoice,
for the Lord will do great things!
—Joel 2

For he has chosen the weak and despised
of this world to shame the great.
—1 Cor. 1

He is able to raise up stones and to make
from them children of Abraham.
—Luke 3

And if these are silent, the very stones will speak.
—Luke 19

EPISTLE TO
MARGUERITE DE NAVARRE

To the most Christian princess Marguerite of France, Queen of Navarre, Duchess of Alencon and of Berry, M[arie] D[entière] of Tournai wishes salvation and abundance of grace, through Jesus Christ.

My most honored Lady, just as the genuine lovers of truth desire to know and understand how they should live in these very dangerous times, so we women should know how to flee and avoid all errors, heresies, and false doctrines, whether from false Christians, Turks, infidels, or from others suspect in doctrine, as your writings have already sufficiently shown.[1] And although several good and faithful servants of God have been moved in times past to write, preach, and announce the Law of God, the coming of his son Jesus Christ, his works, death, and resurrection, nevertheless they have been

---

1. The term "false Christians" is very broad and allows Dentière to avoid naming specifically in the title and in this first sentence the particular groups, including the Catholic Church, that she will go on to attack. The rapid growth of the Ottoman Empire, including its invasion of central Europe, made the "Turks" a formidable presence in the Christian West. Dentière's use of the expression "we women" and her reference to Marguerite de Navarre's writing is a rhetorically astute move that associates her with Marguerite and lends authority to Dentière's decision to write and publish on religious subjects. Marguerite de Navarre's *Mirror of the Sinful Soul* [Miroir de l'âme pécheresse] was published in 1531 and in several subsequent editions, including one by Jean Girard, Dentière's publisher, in Geneva in 1539, the year Girard published her *Epistle*. Marguerite's model authorizes the very act that Dentière is performing by writing the *Epistle*, an act that other women can in turn imitate, (see Renja Salminen's critical edition). The *Mirror* was condemned by the Faculty of Theology of the University of Paris in 1533. In 1544, at the age of eleven, Princess (later Queen) Elizabeth of England made a prose translation of the poem. To situate that work in the context of evangelical reform, see Kemp, "Marguerite of Navarre, Clément Marot, and the Augereau Editions of the *Miroir de d'âme pécheresse* (Paris, 1533)"; and Skenazi, "Les annotations en marge du *Miroir de l'ame pecheresse*"; Ferguson, *Mirroring Belief: Marguerite de Navarre's Devotional Poetry*; and Cottrell, *The Grammar of Silence: A Reading of Marguerite de Navarre's Poetry*. In-depth studies of the poem include Ferguson, *Mirroring Belief*; Sommers, *Celestial Ladders*; and Cottrell, *Grammar of Silence*.

rejected and reproached, principally by the wise men of the people. And not only those servants, but even God's own son, Jesus Christ the just, has been rejected.[2]

That is why you should not marvel if in our time we see [a2v][3] such things happening to those to whom God has given the grace to write, say, preach, and announce the very things that Jesus and his Apostles said and preached. We see that the whole earth is filled with malediction and its inhabitants are troubled, observing among themselves great tumults, debates, dissensions, and divisions, greater than have ever been seen on earth: terrible envy, strife, rancor, malevolence, avarice, lechery, theft, pillage, spilling of blood, murders, tumults, rapes, burnings, poisonings, wars, kingdoms against kingdoms, nation against nation. In short, all manner of abomination reigns: father against son and son against father, mother against daughter, daughter against mother, even as far as one selling the other, the mother delivering her own daughter up to all evils. So much so that there are very few among all the people on earth who really know how they should live, seeing such things happen among people who call themselves Christian. And no one dares to say a word about all this because one person wants one thing to be done, another something else; one person lives a good life (or so he says), another evil; this one is wise, that one foolish; this one [a3r] thinks he knows, the other knows nothing; one claims this is good, another that. In short, there is only dissension, and one or the other must necessarily be living in evil, be-

Eph. 4   cause there is only one God, one faith, one law and one baptism.[4]

However, my most honored Lady, I wanted to write you, not to teach

---

2. Dentière alludes to Calvin and Farel's banishment just one year earlier by the Council of Two Hundred, whose members she calls "the wise men of the people." The paradox of the wise and the foolish, found in Ecclesiastes and Paul's First Epistle to the Corinthians, was often cited by the reformers. They argued that the true Christian life looks like folly to the worldly wise and that self-proclaimed wise men were really fools. Erasmus developed his *Praise of Folly*, first published in 1511, around that paradox. Dentière returns to it several times in the *Epistle*.

3. Following the early printers' convention of signatures, I use the notation [a2v] to show where the reverse side [v] of the second leaf [2] of the first gathering or quire [a] begins. See "Note on the Translation." The title page, which usually shows no signature, would be [a1r] or simply [a]. The biblical quotations are on [a1v], and the text begins on [a2r].

4. The series "un Dieu, une Foy, une Loy, et un baptesme" is an echo of Paul's Epistle to the Ephesians 4: 4–6. In verse 5, Paul says: "one Lord, one faith, one baptism." Dentière adds "one law." Her wording would make the reader, especially the sister of the king, think of the French adage: *une foi, une loi, un roi* (one faith, one law, one king). Dentière uses Paul to correct the adage by replacing the king with God, thereby reminding Marguerite and her wider audience that the king is in the service of God and that religion is not subordinate to the monarchy. That message was particularly significant in the late 1530s, when Francis I had authorized severe religious repression and persecution. In the following sentence Dentière urges Marguerite to intervene and use her influence with her brother.

you, but so that you might take pains with the King, your brother, to obviate all these divisions which reign in the places and among the people over whom God commissioned him to rule and govern. And also over your people, whom God gave you to provide for and to keep in order. For what God has given you and revealed to us women, no more than men should we hide it and bury it in the earth. And even though we are not permitted to preach in public in congregations and churches, we are not forbidden to write and admonish one another in all charity.[5] Not only for you, my Lady, did I wish to write this letter, but also to give courage to other women detained in captivity, so that they might not fear being expelled from their homelands, away from their relatives and friends, as I was, for the word of God. And principally for the poor [a3v] little women [*femmelettes*] wanting to know and understand the truth, who do not know what path, what way to take, in order that from now on they be not internally tormented and afflicted, but rather that they be joyful, consoled, and led to follow the truth, which is the Gospel of Jesus Christ.[6] [And also to give courage to my little daughter, your goddaughter, to give to the printers a little Hebrew grammar that she has made in French for the use and profit of other little girls, above all, for your daughter, my Lady the Princess, to whom it is directed. For as you well know, the female sex is more shameful than the other, and not without cause. For until now, scripture has been so hidden from them.][7] No one dared to say a word about

1 Tim. 2

5. Dentière introduces here at the outset the traditional Church injunction against women preaching. She makes a distinction between women preaching publicly and women teaching each other in private. The marginal reference to 1 Timothy 2:11–12, identifies the biblical source (along with 1 Corinthians 14:34–35) of the injunction against women preaching in public: "Let the women learn in silence with all subjection. I suffer not a woman to teach, nor to have authority over the man; but to keep silent." Dentière's life often ran counter to that passage. Calvin's 1546 letter records that she did teach publicly, and the Swiss reformers complained more than once that she had detrimental authority over her husband, Froment. Natalie Zemon Davis has suggested that Dentière's claim to address herself only to other women was a "modest fiction"; see the chapter "City Women and Religious Change," in her *Society and Culture in Early Modern France*, 82–83. The report of Dentière's encounter with Calvin in Geneva supports Davis's view. Her preface to Calvin's sermon on 1 Timothy 2 is her final paradoxical association with those verses.

6. Dentière describes an intended audience consisting only of women. She encourages women converted to the Reformation to leave France as she did. Her husband referred to her as having been expelled from her homeland, but no known evidence records that she left other than voluntarily (see the introduction). Marguerite would be implicitly included among those women whom Dentière urges to follow her example and leave their "captivity" in France. Thomas Head examines the situations and beliefs of the women Dentière refers to here in "The Religion of the *Femmelettes*."

7. The passage within brackets appears only in the copy of the *Epistle* held by the Bibliothèque Mazarine in Paris. Dentière appeals to Marguerite as her daughter's godmother and offers the Hebrew grammar that her daughter has written as a gift to Marguerite's daughter Jeanne.

it, and it seemed that women should not read or hear anything in the holy scriptures. That is the main reason, my Lady, that has moved me to write to you, hoping in God that henceforth women will not be so scorned as in the past.[8] For, from day to day, God changes the hearts of his people for the good. That is what I pray will soon happen throughout the land. Amen.

[a4]DEFENSE OF WOMEN

Not only will certain slanderers and adversaries of truth try to accuse us of excessive audacity and temerity, but so will certain of the faithful, saying that it is too bold for women to write to one another about matters of scripture. We may answer them by saying that all those women who have written and have been named in holy scripture should not be considered too bold. Several women are named and praised in holy scripture, as much for their good conduct, actions, demeanor, and example as for their faith and teaching: Sarah and Rebecca, for example, and first among all the others in the Old Testament; the mother of Moses, who, in spite of the king's edict, dared to keep her son from death and saw that he was cared for in the Pharaoh's house, as is amply declared in Exodus 2; and Deborah, who judged the people of Israel in the time of the Judges, is not to be scorned. Judges 4. Must we condemn Ruth, who, even though she was of the female sex, had her story told in the book that bears her name? I do not think so, seeing that she is numbered among the genealogy of Jesus Christ. [a4v] What wisdom had the Queen of Sheba, who is not only named in the Old Testament, but whom Jesus dared to name among the other sages![9] If we are speaking of the graces that have

Matt. 1
1 Kings 10
Matt. 12

William Kemp and Diane Desrosiers Bonin have explored the ramifications of that passage and cast new light on Dentière's biography in "Marie d'Ennetières et la petite grammaire hébraïque."

8. Dentière's appeal to Marguerite to further the cause of women's learning and writing joins a tradition in works by early modern women. In the dedicatory epistle of her 1555 *Works*, the Lyonnaise poet Louise Labé urges Clémence de Bourges to help her in her efforts to raise women's aspirations "above the bobbin and the spindle" (Labé, *Louise Labé: Oeuvres complètes*, 41–43).

9. Dentière follows here the literary tradition of illustrious women, limiting her catalogue to women in the Bible. See the series editors' introduction to this volume, xix–xxi. Agrippa also names women of the Bible as examples, but he cites many of them as examples of beauty rather than of virtue (*Declamation on the Nobility and Preeminence of the Female Sex*, 52–54, 85). The list begins with Old Testament women.

Sarah was the wife of Abraham and ancestress of Israel (Genesis 11:29–22). She figures prominently in the story of the covenant, the promise God made to the Jews that they were his chosen people. She was initially sterile but when very old gave birth to Isaac. Rebecca became the wife of Isaac and the mother of Jacob and Esau (Genesis 24–28).

The mother of Moses is not named in Exodus, the book that recounts the Jewish captivity in Egypt and eventual escape from bondage under Moses' leadership. In Exodus 2 his mother hid

been given to women, what greater grace has come to any creature on earth than to the virgin Mary, mother of Jesus, to have carried the son of God?[10] It was no small grace that allowed Elizabeth, mother of John the Baptist, to have borne a son miraculously after having been sterile. What woman was a greater preacher than the Samaritan woman, who was not ashamed to preach Jesus and his word, confessing him openly before everyone, as soon as she heard Jesus say that we must adore God in spirit and truth? Who can boast of having had the first manifestation of the great mystery of the resurrection of Jesus, if not Mary Magdalene, from whom he had thrown out seven devils, and the other women, to whom, rather than to men, he had earlier declared himself through his angel and commanded them to tell, preach, and declare it to others?[11]

  Matt. 1

  Luke 1
  John 4

Even though in all women there has been imperfection, men have not been exempt from it. Why is it necessary to criticize [a5] women so much,

---

him to save him from the decree that all male Jewish babies be murdered. She put him in a basket among the reeds on the river bank, and his sister Miriam watched as the Pharaoh's daughter found him and took pity on him. Miriam proposed her mother as a nurse for the baby, who grew up as the adopted son of the Pharaoh's daughter.

Deborah was a prophetess and Judge of Israel who accompanied the Israelite army into battle and urged them to victory over the Canaanites, a people who had oppressed them for twenty years. Her story is told in Judges 4–5.

In the Book of Ruth, Ruth, a Moabite woman, chooses to return to Judah with Naomi, her Hebrew mother-in-law, when both women are widowed in the country of Moab. Ruth embraces Naomi's people and their religion.

Jesus refers to the Queen of Sheba in Matthew 12:42. In 1 Kings 10, she comes from afar to seek wisdom from Solomon, whose reputation had spread to her land.

10. For much of the Middle Ages the Virgin Mary had been an object of veneration as the mother of Jesus. Catholic Church custom had attributed to her an important role as mediator in the process of salvation. Most reformers rejected that teaching, insisting that Christians needed no intermediary in their relationship to Christ. See Warner, *Alone of All Her Sex*.

11. New Testament women include Elizabeth, the cousin of Mary and wife of Zachariah. In Luke 1, the angel Gabriel tells Zachariah that she will conceive a son called John, although she has been childless for many years. John 4 tells the story of the Samaritan woman who granted Jesus' request for water as she was drawing water from a well. In their ensuing conversation he revealed that he knew details of her private life. She believed him when he said he was the Messiah, and she went into the town and told the people of their encounter, bringing them back to hear him.

Mary Magdalene is named several times in the Gospels. Luke 2:2–3 and Mark 16:9 include her among women whom Jesus had healed of evil spirits, "Magdalene, from whom seven devils had gone out." She is next named among those standing at the foot of the cross (Mark 15:40; Matthew 27:56; John 19:25; Luke 23:49). She is among the women to whom Christ first revealed himself after the Resurrection; Luke 23:55–24:12; Matthew 28:1–10; and Mark 16:9, which specifies, "he appeared first to Mary Magdalene, from whom he had cast out seven demons." John 20:1–18 concurs and says Jesus instructed her to go and tell the disciples that he had risen and would ascend to his Father. Dentière and others used this passage to argue that Christ himself had authorized women to preach.

seeing that no woman ever sold or betrayed Jesus, but a man named Judas?
Who are they, I pray you, who have invented and contrived so many ceremonies, heresies, and false doctrines on earth if not men? And the poor
women have been seduced by them. Never was a woman found to be a false
prophet, but women have been misled by them.¹² While I do not wish to
excuse the excessively great malice of some women that goes far beyond
measure, neither is there any reason to make a general rule of it, without exception, as some do on a daily basis. Take in particular Faustus, that mocker,
in his *Bucolics.*¹³ When I see those words, of course I cannot be silent, seeing
that they are more used and recommended by men than the Gospel of Jesus,
which is forbidden to us, and that that teller of fables is well regarded in the
schools. Therefore, if God has given grace to some good women, revealing
to them by his holy scriptures something holy and good, should they hesitate to write, speak, and declare it to one another because of the defamers of
truth? Ah, it would be too bold to try to stop them, and it would be too foolish for us to hide the talent that God has given us, God who will give us the
grace to persevere to the end. Amen.

[a5v]EPISTLE

1 Tim. 2   The Lord God desires that all without exception come to the pure and true
Mark 5   knowledge of truth through one mediator, Jesus Christ alone, by asking for
Matt. 7   that understanding only through a true and living faith, without wavering
nor seeking anyone but him, in whom resides all wisdom, prudence, gen-
erosity, and virtue, to bring down all those who rise up against him and his
Isa. 4   followers, trying to destroy him by tyrannies and human powers. We must
Matt. 10   not fear them, since we have such a great King and master who governs all by
Mark 4   his providence and wisdom, who will halt all winds, storms, tumult, dissen-
Matt. 22   sion, and debates when it is his good pleasure, even though his adversaries
Ps. 109
Heb. 10   come to plot against him. For his enemies must be ground under his feet so

12. Agrippa makes the same argument about men in *Declamation,* 64–65.

13. Fausto Andrelini (1462–1518) was an Italian humanist and neo-Latin poet who studied in
Bologna and Rome before going to Paris, where he was appointed to lecture at the university in
1489. He was a poet at the court of the French Kings Charles VIII and Louis XII. His *Bucolica* or
Eclogues was printed in seven Parisian editions between 1501 and 1515. It is difficult to determine
what lines in that collection of autobiographical and circumstantial verse would have prompted
Marie Dentière to single him out above others for his remarks against women. However, in his
Distiques, two-line epigrammatic poems, there are several lines that might well have offended her
by their sexual and misogynistic content. Dentière may have confused the two works. See *Contemporaries of Erasmus,* 1: 53–56; and Mustard, ed., *The Eclogues of Faustus Andrelinus and Ioannes Arnolletus.* I thank William Kemp for sharing his findings on Andrelini with me.

that the Ethiopians and kings of the earth adore him, and his enemies will   *Ps. 71*
prostrate themselves before his face and will lick the earth. Therefore you   *Isa. 4*
must not be astonished but take courage when you see wars, plagues, and
famines on the earth, nation against nation, kingdom against kingdom, fa-   *Matt. 24*
ther against son, [a6] mother against daughter, one seized in the field and another left, one seized at the mill and the other spared, one taken in bed and
another spared, and so many sects reigning everywhere and others springing
up. For surely that is the moment when the Son of Man will come in great
virtue and power to render to each one his due, calling his Father's elect to his
kingdom, which has been prepared for them since the beginning of the
world.

Be therefore vigilant and ready in tribulation, for you will certainly be
hated by all because of me, led before kings, princes, and lords because you
give witness to truth in my name.[14] And they will put several of you to death,
thinking that they are making a great sacrifice to God. For the elect the days
will be shortened. I foretold it to you: As they have persecuted me, so they
will persecute you. The servant is not greater than his lord. But be glad and
exult, because you are happy when men speak ill of you because of me. Take
courage; because I have defeated the world, you will defeat it. Be on your
guard and vigilant so that the adversary will not find you sleeping. Nothing   *2 Pet. 3*
has happened to me that has not been [a6v] predicted; likewise, nothing will
happen to you that has not been predicted. They held me in hatred without
cause; they will do the same to you. It was prophesied about me; so it is about   *John 15*
you. It was accomplished in me; so it will be in you. And therefore I warn you   *Pss. 68, 118, 119*
to be on your guard, for if the father of the family knew that someone was
supposed to destroy his house by night, he would keep watch and would not   *Matt. 24*
let his house be ruined. And you, unless you are totally out of your mind,
shouldn't you keep watch even more, seeing that the matter is greater, that it's
a question of something much greater than a house?

But we are so blind because of our avarice, which is the root of all evil,   *1 Tim. 6*
that we do not know how to recognize the truth of his words. If it is pointed
out to us well enough, then we can recognize it, but by false doctrines and
long orations, false prophets have seduced and tricked the poor people, letting it be understood that they are christs and saviors of the people. They   *Matt. 7*
walk about in long robes and sheep's clothing, but inside are ravishing   *Luke 20*
wolves.[15] They forbid marriage and foods which we should accept with   *2 Pet. 2*

---

14. Beginning with this sentence and continuing to the end of the paragraph, Dentière uses the
rhetorical figure of prosopopoeia, presenting the imagined speech of another person, in this
case, Jesus Christ.

15. Dentière is targeting the Catholic clergy here, but her criticism of clerics' long robes will re-

Acts 20
Matt. 24
1 Tim. 4

Luke 17

Rom. 14

Gen. 6, 8
Jer. 17
John 3
1 Cor. 2
Matt. 7

Gal. 1

Jer. 19

Rom. 1
Luke 19
2 Thess. 2
3 Kings 22
Judg. 9

John 10
2 Pet. 2
Heb. 2, 5, 7
Jer. 23
Ezek. 26, 33

1 Kings 3

Ps. 80

1 Pet. 1
Rom. 4
Titus 3
Gal. 2

John 14
1 Tim. 2
1 John 2
Heb. 7, 9

Lev. 14
Num. 29

thanks, or they say that Christ is here or there, which is a very strange and new doctrine.[16] Even if [a7] Jesus Christ had not warned us to be on our guard against them, we should not believe them. For the kingdom of God does not consist in such things, nor in any external or visible observation, but it is within us; it is peace, justice, and joy in the Holy Spirit. The Lord God, knowing well that our nature is prone to evil and inclined toward all sorts of idolatry, inclined to believe, receive, and follow false prophets, warned us not to receive, believe, or hear them in any way, not even if it were an angel from heaven saying otherwise, but to recognize that their teaching is not the Gospel and that we would be held in damnation if we accepted it. In spite of that, we did not wish to obey his voice, but we scorned and condemned his holy commandment, and even worse, we loved the lie more than the truth. Because of that, he let us fall into our senses, our inventions, and our carnal desires. For it is right that he who loves the lie more than the truth should have it given to him. And seeing that we did not wish to receive and recognize Jesus as our true Pastor, Bishop, Sacrificer, Priest, Savior and King, he gave us others, to our confusion, as he did to the children of Israel. Like idolaters, they asked for a king [a7v] and they got one, to their great confusion and extreme servitude. They did not recognize the great blessing that God had given them in the good prophet Samuel; rejecting him, they rejected God and not the prophet. We likewise, being ungrateful, did not recognize the great grace that our God has given us by revealing to us his immutable word, his holy Gospel. By responding with sacrifices and external ceremonies, we have abandoned that which we should receive gladly. With his strong hand he had held back our enemies, but all for nothing. Because we abandoned him, he allowed us to seek salvation and life other than in his son Jesus, who was given to us to purge us and cleanse us of all our sins through his blood, without our having deserved or merited it.

In spite of all that, this good God is ready to take us back again, receive us, and pardon us for the love of his son. For it is impossible that sins be forgiven by means other than through Jesus or that we come to the father except through him. He is the path, the way, the truth, and the life, the sole mediator and advocate between God and men, the sole door of life, the sole host who was prefigured [a8] by the levitic ceremonies and sacrifices, which were given to the children of Israel. However, since Christ came, those shad-

---

turn in her later exchange with John Calvin, recounted in Calvin's letter of September 1, 1546 (see the introduction).

16. This sentence introduces three aspects of the Catholic Church that Dentière rejects and to which she will return in the *Epistle*: they forbid priests to marry; they forbid eating meat on certain days; and, worst of all, they believe in the real presence of Jesus in the Eucharist.

ows and figures are past, the spirit is bestowed, things of the flesh are past. *Mark* 15
The letter is dead, and the spirit gives life.

Now we must not serve God in ceremonial, carnal, or visible servitude, *Gal.* 5
but in freedom of spirit. For our God is not carnal nor visible, but spirit; and *Col.* 2
he asks to be adored and served in spirit and truth.[17] Thus, they are all to be *John* 4
greatly reproached who turn us back again to the servitude of external ceremonies through which they have extinguished and annihilated the true evangelical light, attributing to external things that which belongs solely to our
savior Jesus, who, after he had died for our sins and risen for our justification, *Rom.* 4
ascended into heaven visibly and manifestly and is seated at the right hand of *Mark* 16
his father, until he will come to judge the living and the dead.[18] This was *Acts* 1
given to us to understand: that through external and visible baptism, we have
a true and living faith, our sins are forgiven, and grace and justice are given to
us. This [a8v] cannot come about except through the one savior Jesus,
through the spotless lamb who takes away the sins of the world, so that it
pleases the father through his Holy Spirit to draw us to him and together
with Jesus Christ his son.

It was not enough for the wickedness of men to attribute and bestow the
honor that belongs to Jesus Christ on those visible things that were ordained
by God, but also on things ordained and invented by men, without the authority of scripture, such as pilgrimages and money given for indulgences,
and pardons, and a full lot of other evil idolatries that men have discovered,
created, and invented through their good intentions, or rather to pillage and
rob the poor people, going against the holy word of God. It has reached the
point where the earth is filled with idolatries, and if God did not intervene, it
would not be within human power to extirpate and tear them out.[19]

But I pray you, who could sufficiently tell, write, and express the great

---

17. The reformers associated the letter of the law with the ritual ceremonies and levitic regulations of the Old Testament that often involved the body: dietary regulations and cleansing rituals, for example. They taught that Christ had replaced the Old Law with the Spirit.

18. Dentière paraphrases a portion of the *Credo*, the prayer that summarized Christian beliefs.
Two of the best-known creeds, the Apostles' Creed and the Nicene Creed, were formalized in
the fourth century. They were seen to encompass the essential tenets of early Christian faith in
contrast to the subsequent doctrines, laws, and devotional practices that grew up over the centuries. Farel wrote a commentary on the Creed in *Le Pater Noster et le Credo in françoys* (1524).

19. The attack on idolatry is a central preoccupation of the *Epistle*. Dentière includes under that
term a broad range of Catholic Church doctrines and pious practices, from belief in the real
presence of Christ in the Eucharist to the use of indulgences and devotion to objects and images.
Those practices attracted charges of corruption because they often involved the exchange of
money. Dentière often compares them to examples of idolatry in the Old Testament. She begins
by evoking a pious practice that had long attracted criticism: pilgrimage. Pilgrimage continued
to be popular in Dentière's lifetime. See Williams, *Pilgrimage and Narrative in the French Renaissance.*

Heb. 10

blasphemy and injury that we do to our Lord, to his very holy death, and to his precious blood that he shed for us, when instead of the voluntary sacrifice that he made and offered once for us, we come again [b1r] daily to offer a visible thing, without soul, for our redemption? That offering, once made, alters, even destroys the pure and holy teaching of Jesus Christ, when, as if swollen and proud in their spirits, they come to invent and contrive such ceremonies and repetitions of sacrifices. It is as if Jesus Christ had not been sufficient to redeem us, and they had to make another redemption, contrary to holy scripture.[20] They turned the poor people into idolaters who adore the bread and the wine as their own God, when God does not abide in things made by human hands. Nor does God wish to be served or adored in things made by human industry and artifice. But you, wiser than God, will make a beautiful image of him out of wood, half of which you will use to cook your stew and warm your flesh and from the other half you will make a God to adore and serve, asking his aid and help. From a little wheat you will make bread, one part you will give to the poor as God commands; from the other, you will make a God to adore, eat, and devour, which is forbidden. Oh, what a servant, eating his master! What service do you do him, what adoration, yet this practice is highly praised, [b1v] defended and upheld. Certainly not by scripture, right or reason, because they want none of it. But it is enough for our masters that it be maintained by force of tyrannies.[21]

20. Dentière focuses her attack on the Roman Catholic Mass. She objects first to the Church's claim that in the Mass, the priest repeats the sacrifice of Christ on the cross. Most reformers, including Luther and Zwingli, rejected that notion, basing their argument on Hebrews 10, which appears as a reference here in the margin of the *Epistle.* Hebrews offers a systematic argument in favor of Christianity's preeminence over Judaism. Chapter 10 argues that Christ's sacrifice abolished once and for all the need for the repeated, ritualistic sacrifices of the Old Testament. In its attack on the Catholic Mass, the *Epistle* joins a series of polemical works in French produced by the reformers in Neuchâtel and Geneva. Francis Higman attributes to Farel the earliest of these texts in "Les débuts de la polémique contre la messe: *De la tressaincte cene de nostre seigneur et de la messe qu'on chante communement";* see Higman, *Lire et découvrir,* 233–88. Marcourt devotes the first article of the *Placards* to attacking the Mass as sacrifice, a notion he calls blasphemous, because the priests presume to repeat Christ's perfect sacrifice in the redemption. Marcourt's *Placards* are reproduced in Higman, *La diffusion de la Réforme en France: 1520–1565,* 72–75. See the introduction to this volume and Elwood, *The Body Broken,* especially 32–55. Calvin later contributed to the polemic over the Mass in his *Petit Traicté de la saincte cene de nostre Seigneur Jesus Christ.* See Higman's edition in Calvin, *Three French Treatises,* 98–130. Higman's introduction to the treatise (17–21) is an excellent overview of the Reformation polemic surrounding the Mass and Communion.

21. The attack on the Mass continues as Dentière characterizes as idolatry the Catholic doctrine of the real presence of Christ's body in the Eucharist. Farel and Marcourt—and later Calvin—rejected that doctrine and insisted that the bread of the Lord's Supper was a sign of Christ's redemption. In the second article of the *Placards,* Marcourt insists, following the Creed, that Christ's body ascended into heaven after his resurrection and that he is seated at the right hand of God. It follows, he argues, that if Christ's body is in heaven, it cannot be in two places at

If you have scripture on your side, blind and leaders of the blind, why do you not show it? Do you fear the light? Of course, he who proceeds in darkness hates the light; while he who has right on his side shows the light. Why don't you do it without using so many swords, without so many wars, without so much persecuting, killing, murdering, burning innocents, good and faithful people whose blood will come upon you and cry out for vengeance against you before God? Or at the very least, since you cannot vanquish truth, which is invincible, we pray you, for the honor of God, kings, princes, and lords, to whom God has given the sword to punish the wicked and protect the good, allow the truth to be preached in your lands and kingdoms, so that you and your poor people be led no longer by those miserable blind men. They are leading you to the slaughterhouse like poor, tied-up beasts. Do you have a nose made of wax, so that they can turn you about every which way? You seem to be completely emasculated, out of your senses, without fear of God. Have you [b2] so little dread that you dare not see and hear the truth about who is right and who is wrong?

John 12

Matt. 23

Rom. 13

Isa. 1

What do you fear from the cardinals and bishops who are in your courts? If God is on your side, who will be against you? Why don't you make them support their case publicly, before everybody? They are just so many doctors, so many wise men, so many great clerics, so many universities against us poor women, who are rejected and scorned by everyone. What good are they to you, I ask you, if they will not show that their cause is good, ordained by God? Will you put up with them and let them dominate you? We say the opposite of what they say; let them prove what they say.[22] We want to show

John 8

once; see Higman, *La diffusion de la Réforme en France,* 73–74. Dentière, like many reformers, accused the Catholics of cannibalism for "making a God out of bread" and then eating that bread. Dentière goes on to condemn as idolatry the pious practice of venerating statues of Christ, in particular the crucifix, an image of Christ on the cross. Many advocates of church reform shared that opposition to images of God as perversions of faith, sometimes violently destroying them. Iconoclasm was frequent in the Protestant takeover of Switzerland, often fueled by Guillaume Farel and his followers; see Eire, *War against the Idols,* especially 89–94 and 119–25.

22. This passage gives an excellent example of Dentière's skillful rhetoric. She begins by attacking the leaders of the Catholic clergy, the "leaders of the blind," especially for their violence against the reformed believers. She then appeals to those with temporal power over the Catholic hierarchy, the "kings, princes, and lords," to allow the reformed religion (the "truth") to be taught freely and not to be led by those cardinals and bishops. In this sentence she begins with subtle rhetoric to single out Marguerite de Navarre from the others at the royal court and positions her as an audience of one. She uses the phrase "against us poor women," a phrase that, alone, need not include Marguerite. However, she follows quickly with "We say the opposite of what they say; let them hear it." Here again, as in the opening sentence of the epistle, the "we" unites Dentière and Marguerite as women who have articulated their dissident religious beliefs in public writing. Dentière then addresses Marguerite directly and challenges her to be less conciliatory toward the authorities of the Catholic Church. Marguerite de Navarre was criticized

them that they are wrong, let them defend themselves by holy scripture. Have you supported and enriched the evildoers[23] and filled their coffers so much just so they will court you? Have you not done it to uphold the honor and glory of God, [so that they] preach and proclaim his word, show you the straight path, show you how you should live and make your way to resist those who would act or speak against the pure word of God? Yes, of course! But it seems that they are ordained only to play cards, dance, boast, get

1 Pet. 3   drunk, and [b2v] fornicate, which is far from Saint Peter's wish that we be

1 Cor. 3   without crime and ready to give witness of our faith to each other.

That is why, if you are resurrected with Christ, resolve to put your life in

Col. 3   order and search for the things which are above, where Jesus sits at the right hand of God. When we pray to him, our hearts should not be here below, nor should we look at or consider anything visible or temporal, because such things pass away; they are corruptible and transitory. That is why we must lift our hearts on high and think of the things of God, celestial, invisible, and incorruptible. That is why our Lord recommends that in praying we say, "Our Father who art in heaven."[24] Not only should we lift our hearts to heaven toward our father, but also toward Jesus, who is our advocate and brother, who does not want us to believe those who say, "Christ is here; Christ is there." For those whom they want us to think that they have in their hands, in their repositories, and tabernacles are false christs, false prophets, and false redeemers, leading us to believe that they have redeemed us, when they have done noth-

Acts 1   ing. For you must not wait for the coming of Christ except [b3] in majesty,

Col. 3   in power, and in virtue, openly, visibly, and clearly, just as he ascended into heaven. And as it is said: Those who are resurrected with him will look for the things that are above, where Jesus is seated at the right hand of God the father.

---

by some reformers for compromising her religious beliefs by remaining within the Catholic Church. Those criticisms later grew into accusations of Nicodemism, a term coined by Calvin to describe timid witness of one's faith (after the Jewish leader Nicodemus who, in the Gospel of John, chapter 3, came by night to see Jesus). Calvin wrote several letters and treatises against such behavior. His 1544 treatise *Against the Nicodemites* obliquely targeted Marguerite.

23. Dentière makes a pun with the word *maleficiez*, in contrast with *benefices*, gifts or appointments made to the clergy. She turns the word to mean "You do evil."

24. The simplicity of the Lord's Prayer appealed to many people, reformers as well as Catholics. Farel's first published work (1524) was an exposition and commentary of the Lord's Prayer and the Creed, *Le Pater Noster et le Credo en françoys*. Marguerite de Navarre wrote a dialogue on the prayer that closely follows a text of Luther. See her *Pater Noster et Petit Oeuvre dévot*. Clément Marot rendered the Lord's Prayer into a French poem; see his *Oeuvres complètes*, 1: 390. Michel de Montaigne would later write, "If I had my way, on sitting down to table, and rising from it, on getting up and going to bed, and on all particular actions with which we are accustomed to associate prayers, I should like it to be the Lord's Prayer that Christians employ, if not exclusively, at least always" (see "Of Prayers" in *The Complete Essays of Montaigne*, 229–30).

And you must not think that those words that Christ spoke, holy and pure: "This is my body which is given for you; do this in memory of me" create anything other than bread, which we take in memory of the death of Jesus. You must not believe nor imagine that the bread is changed or transformed, transubstantiated into the body of our Lord Jesus, nor that his body comes down from heaven and hides itself under that bread, or with the bread.[25] For that opinion is a crazy illusion and reverie, too superstitious and coarse, and far from the pure word of God and faith of our Lord, through which we believe, expect, and confess our savior to be seated perpetually at the right hand of his father, to come again to judge the living and the dead, his grace, power, and mercy, along with his Holy Spirit, to live and reveal itself in us, until the end of time. Faith, therefore, and the spirit of God residing in us, teach us all of this by the word of God, without [b3v] the illusions of men. For just as circumcision was called the alliance between God and Abraham because it was only the sign that they made in memory of the alliance, likewise, the dove is not the Holy Spirit but the sign of the Holy Spirit that descended upon Jesus when they heard the voice of the father saying, "This is my beloved son, in whom I am well pleased; listen to him." No more than the wind or the tongues of fire are the Holy Spirit, as when they were given at Pentecost, but all of that was the sign of the Holy Spirit. As among the children of Israel, the paschal lamb was called the "passover," the passage made by the angel in the land of Egypt, and baptism, taken in faith, is called the renewal of life in the death of Jesus Christ, because it signifies regeneration and interior spiritual renewal, such that those who are baptized in faith are incorporated at the death of Jesus Christ, as true children in the inheritance, as the good olive is grafted onto the wild olive tree. Likewise, to accommodate us because we are infirm, Jesus Christ is named and called in Scripture by similitudes, not according to what he is, but according to what he represents and signifies. Saint John calls him a [b4] vine, a door and a path; Paul calls him a rock; he calls himself bread. Thus we name and call him bread at the holy table, which is his sacrament. In the same way, the bread is named and called the body of Jesus Christ, because bread signifies and represents the body of Jesus, which was delivered up and put to death for us; it is taken in memory and recognition of his body having been put to death for us. For eating the flesh and drinking the blood of Jesus Christ is a very different thing from taking the bread and drinking from the chalice. The latter is common to the good and the wicked alike; but eating the flesh and drinking the

Matt. 27
Mark 14
Luke 22
1 Cor. 11

Gen. 17

Matt. 3
Mark 1
Luke 3
John 1

Acts 2
Exod. 2

Rom. 9

John 15
1 Cor. 10

1 Cor. 11

---

25. The doctrine of transubstantiation taught that the priest changed the communion host into Christ's body by the words "this is my body" during the consecration of the Mass; see above, nn. 20, 21. The third article of Marcourt's Placards mocks that doctrine.

blood of Jesus Christ is only shared among those who truly have faith. One can easily come unworthily to the table of our Lord, eating and partaking in condemnation and judgment, just as one can unworthily receive baptism— or when without living, certain, and entire faith, a man comes to witness that he is renewed in life and bears witness before the assembly that he is mingled, united, and conjoined with Jesus Christ and then receives exterior and visible baptism to his condemnation, falsely letting it be understood that he is one of the members of Christ. Only interior baptism, however, [b4v] which no one can give except God alone, giving his Holy Spirit, can be received worthily. For it makes the impure and unclean clean and the unworthy worthy, purifying and sanctifying them by faith, giving them his Holy Spirit. Thus, eating the flesh and drinking the blood of Christ is nothing else but believing firmly that our blessed savior gave his body, his flesh, and his life and shed his blood for our salvation. Truly, this cannot be done unworthily and in judgment, but in salvation, for this faith purifies hearts, because Jesus Christ lives through faith in the heart of the believer. Thus eating and believing is the same thing, because we do not have several ways to be saved; there is only one, and that is the faith that we have in Jesus Christ. Saint John the Evangelist makes it clear in several passages, speaking always in the same spirit. In one passage he says it this way: "Who believes in me has life eternal, and I will raise him up on the last day." In another passage he says, "Who eats my flesh and drinks my blood has life eternal, and I will raise him up on the last day." In this we see openly, manifestly and simply enough that faith and eating are said to be the same thing.[b5]

Therefore, in these times we must not look to ceremonies, sacrifices, or visible signs, expecting salvation by exterior and visible things that are administered by men. For if it is the case that man is not justified by works, by the law, nor even by observing all that God commands, but solely by the mercy of God, having faith in his son Jesus, how then will we expect salvation by means of those things which are directly made and ordained by men against God and his word? And therefore we must stop and hold on exclusively to interior goods, to faith, to the spirit opening through charity in our hearts, no matter what the wise proclaim, those who do not yet have the slightest knowledge of the Scriptures, since they settle for visible things. But man must recognize his imperfection, for there is only one who is perfect, in whom resides all perfection; that is Jesus Christ, the just, without whom we cannot have true and perfect understanding of his Scriptures. That knowledge is revealed little by little to his followers, in order that it be understood and declared completely and entirely. For just as by hypocrisy and the force of tyranny that knowledge was extinguished and suffocated for a time, so by the virtue and power of the sword of the spirit of God it will be illuminated and revealed, [b5v] no matter what the tyrants do. For Jesus Christ risen from the dead is clad in glory, and, certainly, heaven and earth must pass away be-   *Matt.* 24 fore a single word of God's word will pass away. And since he promised to be our God and father, he will treat us like his children because we are sons and   *Luke* 8 brothers of Jesus. And we must not doubt that we are heirs and share the in- heritance with him, seeing that he made himself known to us, desiring that   *Matt.* 24 his Gospel, which is the good news, be preached and read aloud throughout the world. He revealed his grace to us, and he will give a fuller understanding to us, but not without persecution. He is true to his promises, and he does not lie as other men do. Who has ever been betrayed by him? Did not Abraham and the other good patriarchs obtain what he promised? Did he not give himself to us in the time he ordained, as he had promised? Who could re- proach him for anything? Why then do we doubt his promises, as if he were not all-powerful? Do you fear that there is something he cannot do? Where is your faith? Does he not hold everything in his hands? What would men do without him? Would the sun set before its time? Would the rain [b6] go back up in the heavens?[26] Yes, much more will happen and more easily than that the Gospel will not spread throughout the world.

Use all your power, tyrants; break your heads against the rock, you will accomplish nothing, beadles of the pope, except breaking your heads; you will be crushed. For in killing and burning the body, you have no power over the soul. Are not the hairs of our heads all counted? Not one will be lost   *Matt.* 6 without the good will of our father, who cares not only for us, but for the least thing that lives on earth, even the birds in the sky. How much more will he look after his children! If his will be such that he lets us fall into the hands of enemies, must we resist his orders, or murmur against him? Why, therefore, do you resist his will and his order, which is not yours to avoid, seeing that the sky, the earth, the sea, and all things in them are created by his word alone? He spoke, and it was done. And you, worm of the earth, poor miser-   *Gen.* 1 able creature full of sin and iniquity, will you undo that which has been made and ordained by such a Prince and King of all things? Will you resist his will,   *Rom.* 3 saying, "Why did he do this?" Will the work say to him who has made it: [b6v] "Why do you make me like this?" Is it not the will of the potter to make one pot to his honor and another to his dishonor, without the work rising up against its master? And you, poor creature, who are even more worthless by   *Rom.* 9 comparison with this great father God than is the pot compared to the pot- ter, in spite of all this, will you fear men and fear to confess Jesus Christ and

---

26. This is the rhetorical trope of *adunata*, or the positing of impossible phenomena.

his word before kings, princes, and lords who are nothing compared to him
Isa. 5   but wind and smoke, or a flower before the sun that is quickly dry and wilted
for all its glory and beauty? Is Solomon in all his wisdom, wealth, and pomp
anything other than dust? Samson, I ask you, with all his strength, Goliath,
with his might, what are they if not demolished by him whose arm is all-
powerful?[27] How can they glorify themselves? Are they wiser, richer, and
more powerful and virtuous than he who destroyed and annihilated? Let
them show their force, and the God of force will destroy them if they do not
return and render thanks to God, who by his mercy gives them grace, so that
Eph. 2   the poor people might come and recognize only one God, only one law and
1 Tim. 2   one faith, a mediator and an advocate, one savior, [b7] and one baptism, leav-
1 John 2   ing their faults and errors, being no longer in so many divisions and dissensions, as they are at present throughout the land.

There is certainly great division among men at present. Some say one
thing; others something else, so much so that the poor people do not know
where to turn. Certainly, either one side or the other must be in the wrong.
For the kingdom of God cannot be divided; it is peace, justice, and joy in the
Holy Spirit. Not the worldly, hollow peace of men, but the peace of God,
Dan. 12, 4   who is in those of us who know his word, before which all must stop, without
Apoc. 22   adding or taking away anything. For without the word of God, we can never
reach the true unity of faith. We must submit totally to it and not to whatever
Luke 16   seems beautiful or good to us, but which is an abomination before God. And
we must not take glory in the multitude of men, in the wisdom of men, in past
times, in our fathers and predecessors. In none of that can we take glory, for
Ezek. 20   the Turks, who are so numerous, say that they believe in one God who made
2 Chron. 30 heaven and earth, the sea and all things in it, governing [b7v] all by his power
Jer. 16   and wisdom. And beyond that, they have the Mohammedan law, that is, the
Lev. 18   Koran of Mohammed, believing that it is holy law, pure, good, and divine.
4 Kings 14 They follow it very austerely, being careful not to transgress its constitutions
and ordinances. Nevertheless, they are in great error, like infidels, and thus
have no reason to take glory in their large numbers nor in their observance of
their law. For it is better to follow the truth in small numbers, with the good
servants of Jesus, even if there is only one left on earth, than to follow the lie
in large numbers with the infidels.[28]

27. The complete nothingness of all humans compared to the glory of God is a dominant theme
in Marguerite de Navarre's *Mirror of the Sinful Soul.*

28. Dentière uses the Muslim religion to undermine the Roman Catholic Church's claim to authority based on the large number of its members. The Muslims, too, she argues, have many
followers and faithfully observe their religion's laws, but they are nonetheless infidels. The reformers often portrayed themselves as a small group struggling against the large numbers of the
Catholic Church. Dentière develops that theme in this section of the *Epistle.*

What good is it, I ask you, to those of Jerusalem, to have followed An-
nas, Caiaphas, and Pilate, the Scribes and Pharisees in large numbers, pomp,
and triumph? Would it not have been better for them to follow Jesus and his
Apostles, even though they were small in number, poor, despised, and condemned, than those who were in great numbers, so rich, powerful, and honored by all the wise men of the world. Of course! For you see that in the time
of Noah, a small number was saved in the ark, and the rest of the world
drowned. In Sodom, few people followed Lot; even his wife remained on the
road. Most of Joseph's brothers sought his death. Only two spies were found
good in [b8] Israel; the others led all the people into perdition.[29] In the time
of the great persecution of Tobit, no one except Tobit was found who feared
God. And Mordecai alone refused to adore Haman, that wicked villain,
while all the people adored him. Daniel, Azariah, and Hananiah likewise refused to adore the image of King Nebuchadnezzar, who shone among the
idolaters like stars in the sky. One thing is certain, that there are more children of Ishmael than there are of Isaac, more of Abraham and Hagar than of
Abraham and Sarah. For it is always a small number that follows goodness,
and a multitude evil. Only the children of Judah followed the house of David
in Israel. A large number followed false prophets, but only a few went after
Elias and Micah. Four hundred false prophets under Ahab and Jezebel served
their god Baal and kept him well-fed, but to maintain the honor and glory of
the Lord, to bring fire down from heaven and show the power of the God of
Israel, Elijah the prophet was alone.

Gen. 7

Gen. 18

Gen. 37
Num. 13

Tob. 1

Esther 3

Dan. 1, 3

Gen. 25
Gal. 3, 4

3 Kings 12

3 Kings 18, 22

The Ottoman Empire had become a major threat to the countries of Christendom. In the
1530s, King Francis I, Marguerite's brother, had been negotiating with the Ottomans in an effort
to win support in his struggle against Charles V and the Hapsburg Empire. In 1534 Francis welcomed the first Ottoman ambassador to France, and the following year the first French ambassador was named to Constantinople. In 1536 commercial agreements were reached between the
two powers. Dentière's mention of the "Turks" may reflect her dismay at the "Very Christian
King" Francis's courting of the "infidels." See Knecht, *Renaissance Warrior and Patron*, 295–96.

29. Several examples from the Old Testament illustrate the argument that the true believers ex-
ist in small numbers. In Genesis 6 and 7, Noah and his family were the only righteous people
among the multitudes of wicked and corrupt on earth; only they were allowed to enter the ark
and to escape the destruction of the flood. In Genesis 18 and 19 wickedness was so widespread
in Sodom that not even ten good men could be found there. Only Lot, his wife, and his two
daughters were allowed to escape before God destroyed the city, and of them, even Lot's wife
perished because of her disobedience. The story of Joseph and the jealous brothers who sold
him into slavery is told in Genesis 37; 39–47; and 50. The two spies refer to Caleb and Joshua,
whose story is told in Numbers 13 and 14. Moses sent twelve scouts, one from each of the tribes
of Israel, into the land of Canaan to spy out the land and report back to the people of Israel in the
desert. They returned to describe a rich land filled with milk and honey. Most of the spies gave
a false report because they were afraid the Canaanites would overpower and kill them. Only
Caleb and Joshua told the truth and urged the Israelites to move into the land of Canaan. The
ten men who returned with a bad report died of the plague, while Caleb and Joshua lived.

That is why it is a great folly that shows ignorance of Jesus to use as evidence against us the multitude of the [b8v] Pharisees, and even worse to want to follow them. For there has never been a time when the world did not follow and seek after Barabbas, that is, the great path that leads to perdition. Its followers are many, but few are the followers of the path that leads to salvation. That is clear enough throughout the Old and the New Testaments. In the time of Moses, several came out of captivity under the hand of the Pharaoh to enter into the promised land, but of the six hundred thousand combatants, there are only two who entered there, Caleb and Joshua. All the others failed to enter the promised land because of their lack of faith, so they wandered in the desert murmuring and going against the commandments of God.[30]

It is certain that many are called, but few are chosen; many in truth are created, but few will be saved. Thus, only a few can truly call themselves Christians, glorifying in God alone. Instead, they call themselves Franciscans, Dominicans, Claires, Marianists, Augustinians, conventists, papists, Anabaptists, and Lutherans, as if they took nothing from Jesus, or as if their derivation were false and they were not baptized in the name of Christ. Certainly all have strayed into error, even we and our fathers, lacking [c1r] the grace and mercy of God.[31]

30. Tobit, Mordecai, and Daniel are all exemplary Old Testament figures of Jews prevailing against those who have taken their people into captivity. In the apocryphal book bearing his name, Tobit remains faithful to God while his people are captive in Nineveh. In the Book of Esther, Mordecai is Esther's cousin and adoptive father who survives Haman's plotting and wins favor with the Persian king Ahasuerus. Dentière conflates two stories from the Book of Daniel. Daniel and his companions Azariah and Hananiah were among the Jews held captive in Babylon by King Nebuchadnezzar. In chapter 3, when they refused to worship the golden image set up by the king, Azariah and Hananiah, together with Mishael, a third companion whom Dentière does not name, were cast into the fiery furnace. An angel appeared with them, and they emerged unscathed. In chapter 6, an angel protected Daniel when King Darius had him cast into the lions' den.

Ishmael is the son of Abraham and Hagar, the slave woman; Isaac is the son of Abraham and Sarah and the father of the Jewish race.

I Kings 17–18 tells the story of Elijah, the most famous prophet of the Old Testament, who killed the 450 priests (or false prophets) of Baal maintained on Mount Carmel by King Ahab of Israel and his wife, Jezebel. Micah was a prophet who foretold the fall of Jerusalem in the Book of Micah.

In Joshua 14, Caleb received the land of Hebron that Moses had promised him for his faithfulness (in Numbers 13–14). Joshua was chosen by God to be the successor of Moses (Numbers 27); he leads the conquest of the Promised Land and its division among the twelve tribes of Israel in the Book of Joshua.

31. Dentière groups together Catholic religious orders, supporters of the pope, and other reformist groups. Differences arose very early among the various groups of reformers. Calvinists and Lutherans disagreed over doctrinal as well as political issues. The Anabaptists were several

And the Jews who were called by Jesus Christ did not wish to recognize him as their messiah and king, but they waited for another one, a carnal, visible, and temporal messiah, who would come in great authority and pomp, with horses, chariots, armies, bastions, bombs, and artillery to ruin, destroy, burn, and murder, having a kingdom that is all carnal and worldly, restoring a carnal and temporal Jerusalem; taking glory in their name, Jews, having scriptures peculiar to them, saying that they understand them and have more knowledge of them than any other nation on earth, as much by the prophets as others who descended from their fathers; having also the promises made to their father Abraham and his seed, from whom they descended, calling themselves the sons of Abraham; believing in one God only, whom they hold in such reverence that they do not even dare to pronounce his name but, instead of saying Jehovah, they say Adonai, the Eternal; striving to keep the law of Moses, the Sabbaths, cleansings, years, figures, and circumcision, even to refusing to eat the flesh of pigs.[32]

Deut. 14

Lev. 11, 12

De conse. Dist. 5.c.2 Carnem

---

heterogeneous groups, originally among the German-speaking reformers but eventually including small groups in other countries. They are so named because they shared a rejection of infant baptism, maintaining that only mature believers should be baptized. They rejected any scholarly or governmental interference in people's religious lives, and they expected the imminent end of the world. They were social radicals who accepted only the vernacular Bible as their authority and insisted on the direct access of ordinary people to divine truth.

32. References to the Jews in the *Epistle* are both positive and negative. The reformers often compared themselves to the Old Testament Jews, a persecuted people in captivity, whether in Egypt or in Babylon. They represented the Church of Rome as powerful negative figures, Pharaoh or Goliath, for example. At the same time they portrayed Old Testament Judaism as a harsh religion of the Law, preoccupied with complicated rituals, in contrast with reformed Christianity as the religion of faith and the Spirit. They reproached the Jews of the New Testament for not recognizing Christ as the Messiah, a reproach that carried over to the Jews who were their contemporaries. Dentière reflects all of those attitudes, and she castigates the Catholic Church for having adopted the ritualistic practices and laws of the Old Testament.

Here and again further on, the frequent abbreviated Latin fragments refer to sections of medieval canon law, authoritative texts of codified Catholic ecclesiastical law issuing from papal letters (called *decretals*), bishops' letters, and Church councils that regulated church government, practices, and discipline. The *Decretum* is a canonical collection compiled in northern Italy around 1140 by Gratian, an Italian legal scholar. The decretals of Pope Gregory IX, composed by Saint Raymond of Pennafort, were promulgated in 1234 and became known as the *Liber Extravagantium* because it was outside the *Decretum*. Pope Boniface VIII issued a collection of laws in 1298; it became known as the *Liber Sextus*, or sixth book, because it added to the five books of the *Liber Extravagantium*. The Clementines are a collection of decretals promulgated in 1317 by Pope John XXII, drawn mostly from the constitutions of Pope Clement V at the Council of Vienne. These became the core of the *Corpus Juris Canonici*, or body of canon law. For a good introduction to medieval canon law, see *Gratian. The Treatise on Laws (Decretum DD. 1–20)*, trans. Augustine Thompson, O.P., with *The Ordinary Gloss*, trans. James Gordley (Washington DC: The Catholic University of America Press, 1993), ix—xxvii; and T. Lincoln Bouscaren, S.J., and Adam C. Ellis, S. J., *Canon Law: A Text and Commentary* (Milwaukee: Bruce, 1958), 1–13. The latter volume provides a key to conventional notation of these early books. The *Epistle* refers to sections of

The pope and his followers do the same on some days [c1v] forbidden by him, still Judaizing as if Christ had never come. It is something very horrible and frightening, a great misery and blasphemy to think, as he com-

dist. 4.c.Deniq. manded in *la dist. 4.chap. Deniq.* that no person dare to eat flesh, eggs, cheese, or milk products for fifty days before Easter. Not only is this commanded of

1 Tim. 4 everyone, contrary to the commandments of God, but also no Carthusian, no Celestine, no Jacobin, no sister Colette, no smoky-browns, Minims, nor other monks may ever eat meat. *de consec. dist. quinta. cap.Carne.*[33] This is ordained by the pope, with all due respect, as are all the other ordinances, with the sole purpose of drawing us away from God. For we order and command that the ordinary man (that is to say, he who earns his living by his work) be so pressured and stressed by pensions and other things that he is forced to withdraw from God. *23.q.8.Iam vero.* And for that reason, the above-mentioned pope has ordered that one tenth of all goods be given to the priests, including wheat, grains, hay, fruits, woolens, fish, flour, wages, and income from all commerce or sale of houses, fields, vineyards, ovens, herds of animals, bees, from hunting or military service—all go to priests' wages.[34] In short, all that [c2] remains is one tenth of the women, although in some

1 Cor. 7 places the priests are so bold as to brag about having them, too; yet it is for-

Nota disti 34 bidden for them to marry as God commanded *à la dist. 34 Is qui.cap.Christiano Si quis non habet uxores habeat concubinas.* Having concubines is allowed, but to

---

canon law by distinction (*dist.*), chapter (*cap.* or *chap.*), question (*q.*), and the first Latin word of the section. I leave the references in their abbreviated Latin notations as they appear in the *Epistle*. I thank Rev. Gerald P. Fogarty, S.J., and Rev. Augustine Thompson, O.P., for their generous help. On the references to canon law in the *Epistle*, see Denommé, "La vision théologique de Marie d'Ennetières."

33. Dentière attacks rules that impose fasting during Lent. The criticism extends to the stricter dietary rules held by many religious orders. The Carthusians are a strict contemplative order whose motherhouse, the Grande Chartreuse, is in the mountains north of Grenoble. The Celestines were a branch of the Benedictine order founded by Pope Celestine V in 1250. The Dominicans in France were known as Jacobins because their Paris convent was on the rue St. Jacques. "Sister Colette" refers to nuns of the Clarisses or Colettine Poor Clares, a reformed order founded in the early fifteenth century by Colette of Corbie. Their convent of Saint Clare in Geneva was the scene of Dentière's efforts, with Farel and Viret, to convert the nuns to the reformed religion in April, 1535, an event recorded by Jeanne de Jussie (see the introduction). The smoky-browns (*enfumés*) refer, because of the color of their robes, to the Cordeliers. The Minims were a relatively new order in Dentière's time, founded by Saint Francis de Paul in Calabria in 1435. Because of his reputation as a saintly hermit with miraculous powers, Francis de Paul was brought to France by King Louis XI in 1483. He became very influential at the royal court, where Marguerite de Navarre and Francis I's mother, Louise of Savoy, were particularly devoted to him. Antoine Marcourt, author of the 1534 placards, gives a similar list of religious orders in his 1533 *Book of Merchants*, also using the word *enfumés* and other words that designate religious orders by the color of their robes. See Berthoud, *Antoine Marcourt, réformateur et pamphlétaire*, 116.

34. Dentière criticizes the practice of tithing, or giving 10% of one's income to the Church.

have a legitimate wife, that smells of fire and rings of heresy. *23 q. 7.cap. Non est. Ex transmissa a nobis pastoralibus, & aux autres cha. De decim. primicijs, & oblationibus.*[35] Since the Jews require more ample declaration, I leave it for the present to those who have worked more thoroughly than I on their language, like Münster in his prologue to Saint Matthew.[36]

Here I am trying only to show Jesus Christ crucified and how he is served in vain and without cause by other means or by other laws and ordinances than his own. We seek salvation only in him, detesting all other constitution and ordinance than his, which is immutable. The mendicant friars say that in truth they live better in their way than those called Waldensians, Picards, or Turlupins, who have existed since the time of the Apostles, fugitives fleeing here and there, because of the great, cruel persecutions they have suffered and continue to suffer, [c2v] straying across the earth like poor wandering sheep without a shepherd. Neither they nor their fathers have ever believed or shown faith in papal law nor in its ceremonies. They have preferred to flee and to endure torments and persecutions than to follow that wicked idol in Rome. I say this so that no one will think it is a new thing to reject papal law, even though I concede that they have erred up to now in some things, for lack of good intelligence, attributing to creatures what belongs only to the Creator.[37] The same is true at present of some Anabaptists, who

35. Another attack on the law of celibacy in the priesthood and on the hypocrisy of priests who take women as concubines while professing to respect the vow of celibacy. In Marguerite de Navarre's *Heptaméron,* stories 60 and 61 portray two such couples. The references in brackets are to canon law (see n. 32 above, second paragraph).

36. Dentière implies here that she has studied Hebrew. Her remark recalls her statement in the *Epistle's* dedicatory address that her daughter has written a Hebrew grammar for the use of young girls, in particular, for Marguerite's daughter Jeanne d'Albret. See Kemp and Desrosiers Bonin, "Marie d'Ennetières et la petite grammaire hébraïque," for a careful review of the continued endeavors of Dentière and her circle in Hebrew scholarship. Sebastian Münster (1480–1553) was a German scholar of Hebrew who taught at the Universities of Heidelberg and Basel. He prepared an annotated translation of the Hebrew Old Testament into Latin in 1534–35. In 1537 he translated the Gospel of Matthew into Hebrew.

37. Dentière expresses sympathy for several dissident groups seen as heretical and persecuted by the Catholic Church. The Waldensians were followers of Pierre Vaudès, a merchant in Lyon who, at the end of the twelfth century, abandoned his wealth for a life of poverty and preaching the Gospel. His disciples, who called themselves the Poor Men of Lyon, were condemned as heretics by the Fourth Lateran Council in 1215. Detractors gave them the name Vaudois, or Waldensians, after their founder. They survived in dispersed, clandestine groups in rural areas, especially in the alpine Dauphiné and Piedmont. Between 1490 and 1530 large numbers of them emigrated to the Luberon region of Provence (see also n. 39 below). See Audisio, *The Waldensians;* and Cameron, *Wadenses: Rejections of Holy Church in Medieval Europe.*

The Picards were a medieval sect so named because they originated in Picardy, a region in what is now northern France and southwestern Belgium. They were harshly persecuted in the fifteenth century in Tournai, the city where Marie Dentière grew up and entered the convent. A

reject and renounce completely and openly the election of God, attributing to themselves power and free will to be able to save or damn themselves, as if there were several saviors or other saviors than Jesus, saying that they have justification by their actions and merits. They establish moreover a new popery, worse than the first one, more dangerous, more cunning, and more sanctimonious than the pope's, given that they stop totally at the faith in Jesus Christ, by whom alone we are justified without our merit and without the

Rom. 3 works of the law.[38] We cannot please God without that [c3] faith. For who-
Gal. 3, 4 ever is under the law is under the [synagogue], and if we are circumcised, Christ is of no benefit to us.[39]

Of course, those poor Christians and faithful have always been forced to be separated from other men, and to hear the word of God in secret, if they wanted to hear it, mostly at night, because of the great persecutions brought against them by those who considered them outside the faith and non-Christian, worse than infidels, denying Jesus and the Gospels. And for that reason, they have called them Waldensians, witches, and poor men of Lyon, saying that they hold wicked services in their synagogue at night, eating their children and doing other dissolute things. A common proverb has grown up around them: *qui tient si tienne*, which means they make no distinction between brothers and sisters, fathers and daughters, mothers and sons, cousins and cousins, which is a false and feigned invention. But by the great tyrannies forbidding people to live by the Gospel of Jesus, they were forbidden to assemble at night to hear the word of God. And because of that they have been victims of such calumnies, and are still being so treated, even in the present, until it will please God to deliver them from it. They have even been forced, under torments, being pulled by [c3v] ropes and having their feet burned by boiling oil to proclaim that the virgin Mary mother of God was a prostitute, and once out of the frightening, horrifying torments, they

---

large number of them fled to Bohemia, where they settled in and around Prague. See Bartos, "Picards et 'Pikarti.'"

The origin of *turlupin* is uncertain. In the fourteenth century the word was used to designate a member of a medieval heretical sect, but it also quickly came to mean a jokester or a rascal. In the prologue to *Gargantua* (1534) Rabelais uses *tirelupin* to designate an unfriendly reader of his book. Dentière ends her sympathetic portrayal of persecuted groups with a disclaimer, acknowledging that they are mistaken in their doctrines.

38. The Anabaptists rejected infant baptism and argued that the sacrament should be reserved for adults. They opposed violence, refused to bear arms and to hold public offices. Led by Konrad Grebel, the group first became prominent in Zurich and then gradually spread to other cities of the Swiss confederation and beyond. Calvin fulminated against them in his "Brief Instruction for Arming All the Good Faithful against the Errors of the Common Sect of the Anabaptists"; see Calvin, *Treatises against the Anabaptists*, 11–158.

39. The text actually reads *pedagogue*, which seems to me in the context a misreading.

say the contrary. But they are quickly tormented and tyrannized again, more than before, so that those cruel people seem to be making them die in order to confiscate their goods. As these past years we have seen examples by that damned monk in Rome, of which things the King has been in the past more fully informed so that he could rectify such injustices, which he will do when it pleases God to give him the grace to do so.[40]

Since we have spoken of all the others, let us come to papal, or in other words, falsely Christian law, without offending anyone if you please, seeing I will speak the truth about it, or at least part of the truth. For it is not in my power, nor in that of any other woman to depict and declare it sufficiently, given its enormity and abomination. I ask you to read and understand before judging.[41] For often people judge without pity or without having read the case, handing down a sentence that deserves an appeal. And yet, if you try diligently to understand, you will find it without comparison stranger and more superstitious, farther from the Christian faith than any other. In spite of that, they are quick to condemn and persecute others. [c4] And yet there is no nation on earth which has erred, blasphemed. and failed in the true and living faith more than they have, they who should invoke the aid of the lord God and humble themselves, recognizing their faults and their sins, asking mercy and forgiveness from him, praying that he will give them the intelligence to understand and know whether what I say is true. But their great pride prevents them from doing that. For they have no desire to humble themselves nor to recognize their faults and errors, no more than the Jews and the pagans confessing entirely and without pretense that they and their fathers have miserably fallen into error concerning the faith of Jesus. Thus, they prefer to remain and persevere in their poverty and misery rather than

---

40. In the early 1530s the Waldensians, associated by the Catholic church hierarchy with the reformers, became the target of persecutions. In 1532 some leaders of the Waldensians met with Farel and other representatives of the Swiss reform in the Piedmont alpine valley of Angrogna in an attempt to resolve their differences. The reformers continued to support them as persecutions increased in the late 1530s. Dentière was well aware of those events. In 1545 Francis I gave in to pressures and ordered the massacre of the Waldensians in and around the Luberon villages of Mérindol and Cabrières. Some 2,700 people were murdered. Calvin reacted with horror in a letter to Farel, writing that "such was the savage cruelty of these persecutors, that neither young girls, nor pregnant women, nor infants were spared. So great is the atrocious cruelty of this proceeding, that I grow bewildered when I reflect upon it. How, then, shall I express it in words?" (*Letters of John Calvin*, 1: 458).

41. The phrase "Read and then judge" (*Lisez et puis jugez*) is found on the title page of the *Very Useful Epistle*. It is a command or an entreaty often used by the Neuchâtel reformers to ask for a reader of good will, one who will not immediately rush to judgment against the writer. The phrase also conveys the writer's confidence in the strength of her argument. See Kemp, "L'épigraphe 'Lisez et puis jugez.'"

diligently to see, hear, confess, and recognize their errors. That is a great
curse of God sent upon them, because they have given more glory and honor
to the creature than to the Creator, serving and adoring the creature more
than God, whom alone we should adore in spirit and truth, and who does not
want us to give his honor and glory to anyone other than him. And nevertheless, he has allowed them to fall into contradiction.[42]

What greater blindness can you imagine than to have believed, followed, and taught the things they themselves make fun of, for example that
holy water extinguishes the fire of purgatory, [c4v] chases away devils, turns
away storms, thunder and winds, and that the salt of baptism given to little
children gives them knowledge and wisdom, and, above all, teaching them
to turn to doctors who cure all ills, like Saint Rock for vomiting, Saint Wolf
for the teeth, Saint Fox for eating, Saint Cosmos for the castrated, and
Damien for the crippled on all sides? There is not a city nor a village that the
pope does not have under his control. One cures cold and another heat; one
the eyes, another the nose; one cures the fingers, another the fingernails.[43] In
short, God has nothing more to do with it. In spite of that, they all declare
and confess one God who created the heavens and the earth, all good, all
wise, all powerful, and all merciful. Without him nothing is possible, and we
must adore and serve him alone in spirit and in truth. He sent Jesus Christ his
only son, our Lord, conceived by the spirit of God, born of the virgin Mary;
without him we can have no access to the father. The son of God had to be
put to death, he who was just and innocent, for us wicked and evil ones, making us pleasing and agreeable to that good father by his death, calling himself
our advocate and our brother, procuring for us the keys to the kingdom, [c5]
so that we could be heirs and co-heirs with him. In spite of all that, by their
actions they quickly denied and renounced him as their God, their help,
hope, consolation, and savior when by means other than him alone they
wanted to get remission for their sins, seeking salvation and trust other than
in him: by works, merits, religions, journeys, pilgrimages, auricular confes-

Rom. 1
Matt. 14
John 4
Isa. 42
2 Thess. 2
Rom. 1

Gen. 1

John 15
John 4

1 John 2

Isa. 53

---

42. Here Dentière aims her criticism directly at the popes and papal law.

43. Dentière ridicules as superstition the Catholic belief in the efficacy of externals like holy
water and the salt used in baptism. She mocks the veneration of saints invoked to cure illness and
the dedication of entire towns to certain saints. Her list of saints plays on the double meanings
suggested by some saints' names. Saint Roch (Rock) lived in the early thirteenth century, the son
of a noble family in Montpélier who renounced his wealth and lived in poverty and ministered
to the sick. He became ill with the plague in Rome and was saved by a dog who brought him
bread. Saint Loup or Lupus (Wolf) was a seventh-century bishop of Sens. Cosmas and Damian
were twin brothers martyred in the early fourth century. Physicians, they accepted no money for
their care of the sick. Saint Renard (Fox) completes the group, calling to mind Renard the fox,
trickster hero of the medieval cycle of tales *The Romance of Renard*.

sion, masses, adoration of idols, money given for indulgences and pardons and all kinds of other inventions, ceremonies and sacrifices that men have contrived—when it was by one sacrifice only and one oblation only that he sanctified us for all eternity. Will he not be excommunicated by the pope, by   *Heb. 9* that great Melchizedek God of Earth, and rejected by his church, he who will leave his sect to take on Jesus and who will contradict in any way his papal seat?[44] Yes, certainly, not only to him (who is neither God nor man) being above all people and kingdoms, as he says in the gloss of the proem of the Clementines, where it is said, *Papa admirabile.*[45] But also simply to contradict his servants. *In sexto de penis cap. Felicis recordationis, et 17 q.4. Si quis suadente.* Or, what is worse, if it happened that some poor woman had a single goat to feed and [c5v] give milk to her little children after her husband had died, to comfort and console her, would it not be necessary for her to sell it or give it up to pay the offering? Because otherwise, let us denounce as excommunicated as infidels, all those who do not pay their offering. *13. q. 2. Qui oblat.* And even though he himself forbids it by his own books, nevertheless, all of his followers do it, so that there is not one of his priests, bishops, and all those who do his work who would not be excommunicated by him. For he excommunicates all those who give and take something for grace, orders, and such nonsense. *Anathema danti et recipienti, 1.q.1.* That is to say, a curse upon him who gives and him who takes; they should not receive anything for orders or for chrism, baptism, anointing, burial, or communion. *1.q.1,* not even when people would try to force them to take something, *13.q.2. postquam precio.*

But it would be a matter of little concern if there were no other excommunication to fear more than his. For there is, indeed, another, which is proclaimed by a greater bishop, that is, by Jesus Christ and his Apostles, in Acts, chapter 8, against those who think they have—or want to have—God's gifts for gold or silver, and not [c6] by the grace and mercy of God alone, God who wants us to learn from him to be benign and courteous, giving without   *Matt. 11, 10* receiving anything in return.[46] For we received his grace for nothing. He   *Matt. 18* took back our brothers in all kindness, leading them to the true fold of his   *John 11* church, forgiving them just as we want our father in heaven to forgive us, ad-   *Matt. 6*

44. In Genesis 14, Melchizedek was a king of Salem and priest of the Canaanite cult who blessed Abraham in the name of "the most high God" and offered him bread and wine when he returned from battle. Abraham gave him a tenth of his possessions. Melchizedek is usually seen as a positive, even a messianic figure, prefiguring Christ. Some church writers had claimed that Melchizedek prefigured the pope. Dentière uses his name in that context to attack the popes who demanded a tithe, or tenth part, from the faithful.

45. The following section includes more references to canon law (see n. 32 above).

46. Simony, the sin of buying church offices, is so named after Simon the magician, whose story is told in Acts 8:9–24.

monishing them like brothers, pointing out their faults, as the word of God commands, so that their souls be not lost by our negligence. For the soul will

Ezek. 3

be claimed from our hands, if we do not do what we should. But if they are obstinate in their malice, rejecting the doctrine, the admonitions and the word of God, like dogs and swine, you must not give them holy things or

Matt. 5
Matt. 18

pearls [*marguerites*], lest they ruin them.[47] Instead you must excommunicate them and expel them from the church of Jesus, that is, from the holy congregation of true and faithful Christians, like rotten members, unworthy of the body of Jesus, following always the pure, unfailing word of God.

Getting back to Melchizedek: to Jesus alone are the scriptures attributed and not without cause, for they belong to him alone, because he is the king of

Heb. 7

justice and *rex Salem*, king of peace, without genealogy, without father, without mother, without beginning, and [c6v] without end in that he is God and one with his father. But he who tried to raise himself above God, making

2 Thess. 2

himself be adored like God, dared to call himself Melchizedek, *libr.2 ration. divino. offici.* For it suits him well: he is a good king (if I do not lie) of peace, in stirring up as anyone can see, wars, divisions, and debates between kings, princes, and lords of the earth, great genealogies coming out of apothecaries' drugs, giving the recipe to all those doctors. But what audacity, I ask you, what arrogance is this, calling himself Melchizedek: usurping thus the name of Jesus? We should not be surprised that he also usurped the position of Jesus, the goods of kings and princes of the earth, since he did so to God.[48]

Some might be upset because this is said by a woman, believing that this is not appropriate for her, since woman is made for pleasure. But I pray you to be not offended; you must not think that I do this from hatred or from rancor.[49] I do this only to edify my neighbor, seeing him in such great, horrible

47. Playing on the dictum against casting pearls before swine, Dentière makes a pun. One meaning of the word *marguerite* is "pearl." Marguerite de Navarre was known as the Pearl of the Valois. Dentière warns Marguerite not to compromise herself by giving in to the Catholic hierarchy, the "swine" in her analogy.

48. The *Rationale divinorum officiorum* is a liturgical manual written by Guillaume Durand (c. 1230–1296) bishop of Mende in France. The *Rationale* calls the pope Melchizedek, but Dentière protests that Jesus is the only "king of Salem." The word Salem comes from the Hebrew word for peace.

49. Dentière eschews the conventional female writer's modest disclaimer and request that readers forgive her work's shortcomings because she is a woman. Marguerite de Navarre, begins her poem "To the Reader" at the beginning of *Marguerites de la Marguerite des Princesses (Pearls of the Pearl of Princesses* [1547]) with these lines: "If you read this entire work, / Stop, without going further, at the matter, / While excusing the rhythm and the language, / seeing that it is the work of a woman, / Who has herself no knowledge, no learning" (36; my translation). Dentière acknowledges that her *Epistle* transgresses even further because it criticizes and therefore displeases men who believed that the role of women was to give pleasure.

darkness, more palpable than the darkness of Egypt.[50] Nevertheless, if it
please you to consult and diligently examine the texts cited here, which are
themselves cited in their decrees, comparing them to holy scripture, with
good judgment, [c7] you will find even more than what I say here. I would
not know how to write and expose the great follies, evils, and blasphemies
that are written in their books and decretals. No man could be able to expose
it enough. How, therefore, will a woman do it?[51] In spite of that, be diligent
in examining carefully the texts and the consequence of what they say, and
you will see that I speak the truth. One consequence is that they have strayed
from the path of Christianity, as you can clearly see from just three reasons
that should move the faithful Christian to flee from evil papal law.

The first is that they renounce the death and passion of Jesus, when by
another redemption they try to claim the poor people, who were redeemed
once and for all by the precious blood of Jesus. Not satisfied with that redemption, they make another one of bread and wine, secretly in their canon.
Who would not feel more than satisfied to have paid a debt once? But wanting to pay off a second debt, they renounce the first one. They cannot give as
an excuse that they do it in memory of the death and passion of Jesus Christ,
because they are liars. They do it in memory of the [c7v] Virgin Mary,
mother of God (as they say), and of Jesus Christ and several others, as is contained in their *communicantes & memorian facientes*, that is, in memory of Clitus,
Grisogone, Cosmos, and Damien.[52]

The other reason is that they not only trick, seduce, and pillage the poor
people, but, worse than Turks and infidels, like mad dogs, they have the enemy and adversary of God adored. They try by their tyrannies to make him
be adored. For just as Satan tried to make Jesus adore him on the mountain,
showing him the kingdoms of the earth and promising to give them to him if
he bowed down and adored him, they try to do likewise to those who would
serve, follow, and honor Jesus. You see it clearly enough in the way that those
who would preach Jesus and his word purely are run out of the courts of

50. Darkness was one of the plagues that God sent to punish the Egyptians when the Pharaoh
refused to free the Jews from captivity; see Exodus 10.

51. Her question conveys ironically her reaction to those who would question women's ability
to examine the papal decrees and compare them to sacred scripture, a task that Dentière under-
takes here in her epistle.

52. Dentière again attacks the devotion to saints and gives four names of saints who were com-
memorated, beginning with the Latin words *communicantes & memorian facientes*, during the canon,
the most solemn part of the Mass. Clitus—or Saint Anacletus—was thought to be the second
successor to Saint Peter as pope and bishop of Rome. Grisogone is a form of Chrysogonus, a leg-
endary Roman saint during Diocletian's reign. Cosmas and Damian were revered as the patron
saints of physicians. All were known as martyrs.

kings, princes, and lords.[53] But in abjuring and returning to kiss the slipper of that great locksmith, adversary of Jesus, they are given benefices, prebends, revenues, crowns, and mitres, and even worse, under the guise of the gospel.[54] It is as if you, queen, and the other princes and lords wanted to support such vermin on earth, something that I cannot truly believe is your intention. But, they say, [c8] someone else would do it anyway, and it is better that I do it than the infidels. For I will preach, I will indoctrinate, I will give good examples, I will make something good from it, rescuing the poor persecuted brethren, and also, he would do no more nor less for me, but nevertheless I

Rom. 3   will be able to grab a bishop's post.[55] O miserable creature! It is right that you be damned for that, doing evil so that good may come from it to your own advantage. Surely Moses, being the first in the house of the Pharaoh, would have been able to find more ways, more excuses, and more reasons than you

Exod. 2   do if he had loved worldly honors; but he preferred disapproval, poverty, and
Acts 7   insults to all the riches of Egypt.[56]
Heb. 11

Therefore, lady, I pray you, avoid them: they are flatterers; they ask only for themselves and not for the things of Jesus Christ. You have maintained and supported them too much. Your great kindness and humanity has spoiled and lost them. There is a great danger that they will spoil you by their flatteries and by their enormous poperies. Which one of them now preaching

Exod. 20   the holy Gospel does not know that images are made and invented in spite of
Wisd. of Sol. 13   God and against his commandments? They are called devils throughout
Deut. 4, 5, 7,   [c8v] the holy scriptures, but they are nevertheless adored and served, cover-
12, 27
Pss. 115, 9   ing themselves with a soft cloth, taking that cover from their heads, saying that they do it to honor God, that these are the books of the poor ignorant people, saying, "We act from good intentions, and we give support to the weak." As if God wanted to be served and honored by those who break his

Deut. 12   commandment and by the fantasy of men! They are wrong, for God wants us

53. The court of kings targeted here is that of Marguerite's brother Francis I, from which evangelical reformers had to flee after the Placards Affair in 1534.

54. The great locksmith is the pope, who, since Saint Peter, has been called the keeper of the keys to the kingdom of heaven. Kissing the pope's slipper was a mark of reverence. In 1538, Marguerite accompanied Francis to meet Pope Paul III in Nice. Dentière implicitly criticizes Marguerite and attacks those who renounced their reformed position and returned to the Catholic faith in order to receive benefices.

55. Marguerite de Navarre was criticized by some reformers for compromising her religious beliefs by remaining within the Catholic Church. In 1536, Marguerite had obtained the bishopric of Oloron, a town in her husband Henry of Navarre's realm, for Gérard Roussel, her chaplain, an evangelical reformer who remained Catholic. In that post he continued to work toward reforming the church from within until his death in 1555.

56. The evangelical reformers often compared themselves to the Jews held captive in Egypt.

to do what seems good and beautiful to us, but only so far as he commands us, and he condemns those who would add to his commandments or take away from them. Not content with that, they come with their ceremonies, called, if you wish, vespers or matins, to damn those who make images and all those who have confidence in them. That shows their great damnation, ingratitude, and evil, because in giving to their idols, they condemn the poor people. The poor never receive the gift nor the offering, which goes instead to themselves and their chambermaids. They are like those who sacrificed to Baal in Babylon.

Gal. 1
Apoc. 22

Ps. 115 or 113

Dan. 14

To excuse themselves, they will say, "It is not thus that the law should be understood. David the prophet did not mean us, but the other idolators of his time. Scripture has several [d] meanings, and it can be understood in several ways. It is not up to women to know it, nor to people who are not learned, who do not have degrees and the rank of doctor; but they should just believe simply without questioning anything." They just want us to give pleasure, as is our custom, to do our work, spin on the distaff, live as women before us did, like our neighbors.[57] For she who lives like her neighbor does neither good nor evil. Hah! it is certainly true that many of your people will live like that, giving to scripture many meanings and giving you a bag to fill up.[58] You would certainly understand scripture very well [without them], but even we understand and believe it not only simply but even foolishly. I ask, did not Jesus die as much for the poor ignorant people and the idiots as for my dear sirs the shaved, tonsured, and mitred? Did he preach and spread my Gospel so much only for my dear sirs the wise and important doctors? Isn't it for all of us? Do we have two Gospels, one for men and another for women? One for the wise and another for the fools? Are we not one in our Lord? In whose name are we baptized? By Paul or by Apollo, by the pope or by Luther? Is it not in the name of Christ? [d1v] He is certainly not divided. There is no distinction between the Jew and the Greek; before God, no person is an exception. We are all one in Jesus Christ. There is no male and female, nor servant nor free man.[59] I am not talking about the body, for there is the father and the

1 Cor. 1

Rom. 2
Eph. 6

Gal. 3

---

57. This sentence summarizes sarcastically the stereotypical view of the proper role for women. Spinning and its symbols, the distaff, bobbin, and spindle, are frequently evoked in the literature of Dentière's time either as an appropriate occupation for women or as one that women should rise above in order to pursue more intellectual activities that will give them greater access to power. See Louise Labé's dedication of her works to Clémence de Bourges, "A.M.C.D.B.L." (Labé, *Louise Labé: Oeuvres complètes,* 41–43).

58. Dentière implies that the priests would expect Marguerite to fill the bag with money as remuneration for their services.

59. Dentière draws on the beginning of 1 Corinthians to make her strongest statement about the equality of all men and women before God. Paul does not specify women, but Dentière uses

Exod. 20
Eph. 6

son, one to be honored and the other to honor; the husband and the wife, she to love and the other to hold her in esteem; the master to command, the servant to serve and obey; the king, prince, and lord to rule and judge, the subject to obey, carry, tolerate, and pay tribute, taxes, charges, and rents, ac-

Rom. 13 cording to God's word. The person who resists, resists God.

But what do you think about that? Will all our ancestors be damned? Were not our fathers good men? Have they all failed? We have seen such learned people in the past, leading such good lives, fearing God, as much as or even more than at present. God would be very unjust to have hidden the truth so much from us; hah! he would not have waited so long to reveal it to us and have the knowledge of it spread by women. But what miracles do these men perform that our own have not performed? Since they arrived, we have had only wars, dissensions, and debates against one another, famines, malevolence, and bad times. Why [d2] then would we believe something other than we believed before? Before this we came and went in safety throughout the world, honored, cherished, and loved by everyone. Now we do not dare to leave our houses and our towns to do our work or collect our goods, because some people are persecuted and put in prison, while others are burned, tyrannized, and put to death. It has reached a point where no man can dare even to visit his wife and children, which is a pitiful situation caused by the enemies who have surrounded us. And yet, what should move us to believe them? There are so many great clerics who believe the opposite, so many good people, so many kings, princes, and lords who, if they saw the thing as you do, as holy and coming from God, would gladly follow it. Do you want to be wiser than all of them, than all the universities in the world, than all the councils of the popes? In short, it is impossible that so many good people would have wandered so miserably into error, as you say. We see here,

Matt. 16 faithful Queen, the allegations of the poor blind ones, may God be merciful to them, who, speaking according to men, understand nothing of the things of God, which they always oppose, calling them foolish.[60] [d2v] For it is cer-

---

his argument that Christ is not divided to make her point. When she says she understands the Gospel foolishly, she evokes the paradox of the wisdom and folly in Paul's first chapter and shows that she has understood it very well. Verses such as 1 Corinthians 25: "For the foolishness of God is wiser than men, and the weakness of God is stronger than men," work to the advantage of women, whom men had dismissed as weak and foolish. The second of the four Biblical quotations serving as epigraphs to the *Epistle* might be seen as a motto for Dentière's mission in the *Epistle:* "God chose what is low and despised in the world . . . to shame the strong." (1 Corinthians, 1:27–28) Here and in the passage that follows, she defends the faith of the simple people, the kind of faith she attributes to women and to the reformed religion, against the tyranny of the Catholic theologians who claim authority to define doctrine from their privileged positions in the universities and in papal councils.

60. Dentière brings Marguerite de Navarre into the community of the simple people by ad-

tain that God will destroy the wisdom of the wise and the prudence of the prudent. And so he chose weak things, small and contemptible, to bring down the great. 1 Cor. 1. There are many causes and reasons which would help you to understand why this has been so hidden. One of the main ones which should satisfy you is that when it pleased God to raise up some good and faithful person to declare the abuses and evils of the popes and their followers, the kings, princes, and lords who committed fornication with that great Roman lecheress full of abomination and filth were (it goes against my heart to say so) the minions and satellites to carry out the evil sentence, in order that she be adored and served like God, seating herself in the temple of God as if she were God. Just as the prophet Micah said, it happened: that is, that the prince ordered, and the judge obeyed. They have served and obeyed her so much that they have persecuted the blood of Abel and Zachariah, son of Barach, just and innocent unto death. Now they are persecuting as their fathers did, so much so that a clamor has risen to heaven, crying out for vengeance when you make your judgment, Lord God. O [d3] unhappy conspiracy, o miserable alliance, O damned judgment! What have you done, kings, princes and lords with that great glutton that is Rome?[61] Monuments, why don't you open? Rocks, why don't you split apart? Abysses, why don't you come to swallow up and devour on the spot those poor miserable creatures, Coreb, Dathan, and Abiron?[62] O adherents and supporters of the pope, don't you see that you are manifestly waging a battle against God? You have railed against one another so that God is avenged of his enemies by his enemies. But what you have against him is greater than your differences, because you will never see the end of it, but you will destroy one another rather than the church. And the more you persecute, the more you light that great, consuming fire. The church is at home in the hearts of men; your knives are useless there; they are too tender. It is certain that you despise the true Christian faith, yet you are in no way moved to provide for it. Thus you love to serve the furor of God rather than his kindness. It is clear that you are too

Apoc. 17

2 Thess. 2
Mic. 7

Matt. 23

Apoc. 6

Isa. 1

Jer. 35

---

dressing her directly and emphasizing Marguerite's agreement by the phrases "if they saw the thing as you do" and "it is as you say." The word "thing" (*chose*) is used variously to mean the truth, God's will, or simply, as later in this passage, "the things of God."

61. Micah's prophecy appears in the Old Testament book that bears his name. He attacks the corruption of the religious and political leaders of Samaria and Jerusalem. The image of gluttony was a favorite among the French-speaking Swiss reformers when attacking the pope and the Church in Rome; see Persels, "Cooking with the Pope." The word *gouliffre*, translated here as "glutton," appears in different forms in the 1533 *Le livre des marchans* of Antoine Marcourt, author of the placards against the Mass; see Berthoud, *Antoine Marcourt*, 114–15.

62. In Numbers 16, Korah, Dathan, and Abiram were Levites who led an uprising against Moses and Aaron in the desert. The earth split asunder, and the ground opened up and swallowed the three men and their households. Psalm 106:16–18, refers to their rebellion.

cowardly, too full of Roman venom. The pope is your vassal, and you put up with being his, even to being his lackeys [d3v] in order to lead a beast with you, *dist. 96. Constantinus,* saying that the emperor is the lackey of the pope, and yet he is allowed to ride like the emperor. Are you too blind to see that? The sword of God is yours, and the pope takes it away from you. You are ordered by God to defend and protect the good and punish the wicked, but for the love of the pope, you do just the opposite. For the love of God, leave that

Eph. 5

cruel master and accept good Jesus and his word. Too long have you served him; too long have you obeyed him. Wake up, kings, princes, and lords; you

Rom. 13
2 Thess. 5

have slept too long. Night has gone; day has come. It remains only for you to see it. Have no more hearts like the Pharaoh's, so little moved by pity, so late in caring for your salvation and that of the poor people. If you don't, you will find one stronger than you, whose will you hold in little or no regard, who in these times has wanted to declare his will by those who pleased him, although we did not deserve it, but since you are puffed up and proud, you rejected him. So, if there is some good person fearing God and his holy word, wanting to live only as God commands, without doing wrong to anyone, detesting all idolatry, blasphemy, pride, lechery, and drunkenness, in short, to live as a good man, he will be persecuted and put to [d4] death, because he will not adore the Antichrist by observing traditions that are contrary to Jesus. In spite of all the outrages and insults that they can think of to do to him and his followers, he will scatter all those who rise up against him by the sword of his word, against which they rebel like mad dogs. The oak must lose its leaves in due time and its wood must be put to use so that someone may profit from it. Oh, what cries, what lamentations on earth, seeing such merchants losing their wares of gold, silver, bread, wine, and what's worse, souls.

There is still a general reason behind all of this, which is enough to close the mouths of all blasphemers against the truth. He makes known to his creatures his justice and mercy, to some by his condemnation, as to the Pharaoh, showing his great power through Moses; but the Pharaoh rebelled against God's commandments, even though he saw the great signs and miracles that Moses performed in his presence by God's power, because his heart was hardened. To others he shows his power for their consolation and salvation, without their having deserved it; his goodness and mercy alone give them the grace to recognize it and to have full, perfect [d4v] faith in his son Jesus,

Rom. 4

who died for our sins and was resurrected for our justification. That faith alone justifies us, without the works of the law, making us pleasing to God by

Mark 15

means of Jesus Christ. It also justifies the thief hanging on the cross, Paul persecuting the Christians on the road to Damascus, and Jacob in the womb of

Rom. 9
Acts 9

his mother, loved by God but hated by his brother Esau, without any of them having done either good or evil. The justice and mercy of God is manifest in them.⁶³ And who does all that? Is it not in the power of God to do what he pleases, to raise up and to bring down, to exalt and to humble, to elect and to condemn, to save and to damn, to hold back his word and to give it out when it pleases him? Who, therefore, can take that function away from that great Master, since he decreed it, and since it is his alone to exercise with power, *Isa. 14* glory, and honor? Will it be man, who is only rot and wickedness, to whom belongs only confusion? Oh, you poor creature! You should do nothing else *Dan. 1* but humble yourself and give thanks to that good father of all mercy for that great gift that he has given you in these times of his holy Gospel, [d5] letting you see it when so many kings in times past, so many good prophets wanted to see it but did not see it. They would not have been so ungrateful to receive Jesus and his holy word as we are. So many good people before us would have embraced it, they who only saw in spirit what you see clearly. God may have saved them, not condemning them, as you do, so rashly to be damned; and even if he would condemn them, he would do it in his justice. For if the blind lead the blind, they both fall into the ditch.⁶⁴

Nevertheless, the mercy of God is great, who looks to his son Jesus Christ, through whom the ignorance of humankind is often taken into consideration. And as he says, "If I had not come, you would have no sin; but since I am come, you have no more excuse for your sin." For much more to *John 9* blame is the servant knowing the will of his lord and not doing it than he who does not know it. Nevertheless, it is the master's right to reproach each of them. Obstinate and foolish ignorance is no excuse before God, but it is condemned when by a certain malice you resist the word of God, which is declared by his ministers, sent from him and by him, so that there is no human wisdom that can resist them. [d5v]. But even his greatest adversaries must bear witness to their condemnation, saying that it is the work of God and not of men. Openly repugnant to the spirit of God, they will be punished, for their witness is diabolical. And not only them but also those who conspire *John 8* with lies, who ask nothing but to destroy and spoil, swearing to speak the truth. In that, they show clearly that they are the devil's sons, demanding approval for their faith in him, arguing that the mass is good, that God is inside the bread, that they now preach the truth. They argue whether the sheet at

63. The end of the *Epistle* returns to the basic tenet of the reformers' religious belief, that salvation comes undeserved through God's grace and mercy to people who have "faith alone."

64. Christ's parable of the blind leading the blind is told in Luke 6: 39: "Can a blind man lead a blind man? Will they not both fall into a pit?" The image of the blind leading the blind was very popular in the sixteenth century. Peter Brueghel's painting *The Parable of the Blind* (1568) shows a line of six blind men, the first two of whom are falling into a ditch.

Chambéry or the one in Besançon is the shroud of Jesus Christ, which, in imitation of Jesus Christ they should make silent. I don't know how men are so ignorant or so out of their senses and their faith as those men are, turning to the devil, father of all lies, in order to know the truth. Jesus alone is truth, and we must turn to him alone and to no other, and to his word, in order to know it. Look, I pray you, at Saint John in his gospel, chapter 20, and you will find whether bread dough or a sheet is the shroud of Jesus. He is there so well depicted (and on a headdress, no less) that nothing else is necessary.[65] But you will say that so many good people have believed that, and even some dukes of Savoy have honored, [d6] prized, and held it. And what's more, lately, when it was burned in Chambéry, the devil (as they think) speaking through the mouth of a good, learned woman (as the wives of priests usually are; as

the demoniacs of Tournai who were cured by the whip) said it was so.[66] And

65. The cloth known today as the shroud of Turin, believed by some to be the shroud in which Christ was buried, was owned in the early sixteenth century by the Dukes of Savoy and housed in the royal chapel of Chambéry Castle. It was believed to have miraculous powers. In 1532 a fire in the chapel damaged the shroud. When French troops invaded Savoy in 1535, the shroud was taken to Piedmont for safety and exhibited in Turin, Milan, and Nice. The shroud's history and reputation were widely known. In his *Gargantua* (1534) François Rabelais included this detail in his comic description of the enemy being routed by Friar John: "Some called on Saint James, others on the Holy Shroud of Chambéry—but it was burnt three months later so completely that they could not save a single thread . . ." (Rabelais, *Gargantua and Pantagruel*, 100).

66. This convoluted sentence with its parenthetical asides uses irony to relate belief in the shroud of Turin to other beliefs and practices of the Catholic Church: demonic possession and exorcism. I have been unable to learn more about the demoniacs of Tournay who were cured by the whip. The bibliography on demonic possession, often related to heresy and witchcraft, is vast. For a thorough recent study of those related phenomena, see Clark, *Thinking with Demons*. For the region around Geneva, see Monter, *Witchcraft in France and Switzerland*. Studies of women and demonic possession are more frequent for the later sixteenth century than for Marie Dentière's lifetime; the communal demonic possession of the Ursuline nuns of Loudun has generated numerous books and articles; see Certeau, *The Possession of Loudun*. Sluhovsky's "The Devil in the Convent" is an excellent study of mass demonic possession as a gendered phenomenon distinct from witchcraft. The *Malleus Maleficarum* [Witch's hammer], by Heinrich Krämer and Jacob Sprenger, was first published in 1487 and edited frequently during Marie Dentière's lifetime. A manual for inquisitors, its influence has been both argued and disputed. Although whipping was not a technique recommended in manuals of exorcism, whips were sometimes used as punishment when people were suspected of faking possession.

In the margin next to the sentence about the demoniacs of Tournai is printed "Histoire veritable (*True Story*) l'an 1535." In 1510 Thomas Murner, an Alsatian writer and eventual opponent of Luther, published in Strasbourg *Wahre histori von den fier ketzeren prediger ordens der observantz zu Bern Eydgenossen verbrannt kurz nach*, the story of four Dominicans in Berne who deceived the faithful by simulating miracles, including an image of the Virgin Mary who spoke and shed tears. They were tried and executed in 1509. Several editions of the story followed. Lutheran and reformed writers seized on the scandal to illustrate the corruption of the clergy who, through the spectacle of false miracles, sought to exploit the gullible faithful. Thomas More referred to the scandal in "A Dialogue Concerning Heresies," and Erasmus mentioned it in one of his colloquies, "The

not only that, but they also claimed that they were possessed by three devils, that is, by three preachers of the gospel, Farel, Viret, and Froment. Those reasons should be sufficient enough for believing that it is the shroud of Jesus, that the devil is real, and—for people who have no God—that they have led a good life. I ask you, miserable creature, is there anyone wiser than God, more truthful than his word? Why don't you stop there and not at the enemy of God? If those who turn to divination are by the law condemned to death, how much more so will these men deserve death? For if those who turn against Moses, under one or two witnesses, die, what will become of those who scorn Jesus, who is much greater than Moses? Especially those who call themselves leaders of the people, like bishops, priests, monks, preachers, and others calling themselves the light of the world. They take seriously only their stomachs, having great bishoprics and prebends, having no concern [d6v] except for themselves, knowing well that they are not qualified for such *1 Tim. 3* offices. In order to support their dogs, horses, rogues, and bawds and to fill *Titus 1* their stomach, which is their God, they hold posts as pastors, but they are only wolves and wasters, wanting to dominate the people, saying, "It's mine; it's my place, it's my bishopric, my parsonage, who will take it away from *2 Pet. 2, 5* me?" They turn to the arms of the secular to be more at ease and to have their bodily comforts, never considering God's ordinance to be true, thinking it broken by human powers, human commandments, and human orders.

It has come to the point that if anyone contradicts, preaches, or writes against them, he will quickly be judged a heretic, a seducer of the people, a founder of new sects. They must resist them with holy doctrine and condemn them powerfully with the word of God, just as the holy apostle did, and not by swords, banishments, exiles, fire, and insults. In imitation of that apostle, all preachers and ministers must follow the way of God's word, car- *Acts 13* ing for nothing else but that God be glorified and honored throughout the land and that their neighbor be won to our Lord. But Judas must be with Christ, [d7] donkeys must pass under the hearth, lazy bellies reign among the people so that the Prophets can be recognized among the false prophets,

---

Seraphic Funeral." See *The Complete Works of St. Thomas More*, vol. 6.1: 88 and *Collected Works of Erasmus: Colloquies*, 996–1032 and especially 1020, n. 51. A 1549 *Histoire veritable*, published at the press of Jean Girard, the printer of the *Epistle*, is François Bonivard's translation of Johanes Stumpf's *Swiss History*, which recounts the Berne affair (see Higman, *Piety and the People*, S33, p. 373). Given the similarity between the "miraculous" image of Berne and the image of Christ on the shroud of Chambéry, it is plausible that the marginal reference in the *Epistle* refers to one of the numerous adaptations of Murner's account of the 1509 Berne scandal, which Dentière could have first heard about while she was living in Strasbourg and later read in manuscript. The following reference to Farel, Viret, and Froment implies that they were accused of being devils and "possessing" the faithful by their preaching.

truth distinguished from the lie, light from darkness, and black from white. The false will be in great numbers, if they are not already, as much or more than they ever were in the time of Saint Paul, and more dangerous. That apostle complains vigorously that they had seduced and tricked the Galatians, turning them back to circumcision and Mosaic ceremonies already overthrown by the word of God.

And if people complain now about ours throughout the land, it is not without legitimate cause; they have behaved as cowardly soldiers in battle.[67] For when it comes to fighting against the enemies, they are good for fighting, biting, and striking at the table. But when they find themselves in assaults, skirmishes, and ambushes with the enemies of truth (as well as with those who have been expelled),[68] they don't want to bite for fear of blows, insults, and outrages. Thus they are as bold as slugs. That they are not good mercenaries capable of keeping good cities well garrisoned is clear. However, they are strong, skillful, and learned in every way when it comes to feeding their stomachs well, reproaching and blaming those [d7v] who have been forcefully expelled and others who have died in battle.

In all of this, virtuous lady, you must not be surprised if we see such punishment coming from God, because it is only hypocritical monks who are causing all this trouble. That is why such donkeys, wolves, and impudent, lustful hypocrites among sheep should be avoided everywhere and expelled like chimeras from the flock, so that by false doctrine and evil conversation they are not able to seduce the poor people, which is something very dangerous to be feared, if God by his grace does not provide for them, as he has done. For he struck some of them with such force that they fled, and every day more are fleeing, without anyone chasing them, because they know that the judgment of God is on their heads. And above all that poor miserable man, may God have mercy on him, who was not satisfied simply to scandalize the poor people by his false doctrine, but impudently abandoned (if I dare say) his own wife pregnant in Neuchâtel—and, not satisfied with that, returned to his vomitings, so that the mortarboard of the Sorbonnic doctors still smells of garlic. In spite of that, some of his stock, worth little more than he is, are trying repeatedly to canonize him.[69]

67. Here Dentière turns her attack on the current ministers of Geneva, those who had expelled Calvin and Farel.

68. This is a reference to Calvin, Farel, and Coraud.

69. Dentière is particularly acerbic in referring to Pierre Caroli, a follower of Lefèvre d'Etaples who was accused of preaching heresies but was protected by Marguerite de Navarre and given a post in Alençon from 1526 to 1533. Suspected of involvement in the Placards Affair in 1534, he fled to Geneva and eventually became a pastor in Lausanne, where he married. In 1537 he accused Calvin and Farel of Arianism, or denying the divinity of Christ. He was deposed and, abandoning his wife, fled to France, where he received a papal pardon and rejoined the Catholic

[d8] So, to conclude, they are few at present who do not look out more for themselves than for the people of God, providing for men and not for the church of Jesus. Almost all of them are mute dogs, each one eating his bone. It is the best system of government in the world: nothing is lost; all is saved. Welcome hypocrites and all those who know how to please monsieur and madame, who are well-fed and taken care of! One of you is silent, another says not a word, standing by and watching his brothers get drunk. Surely what Isaiah the prophet said has come to be. They have turned back on their *Isa. 56* path, each one to his own avarice. One campaigns for his bishopric; another pleads for his priory; one pities himself; another mourns for himself; one has nothing, another is full; one is hungry; another is drunk; one wants nothing because he wants for nothing. In short, there is only avarice, ambition, and confusion. One comes and another goes without being sent by God, creating division in the church of Jesus. He will destroy both he who pleases and he who wants to please, because we cannot please both God and men; we must *Jer. 6* be loved by one and hated by the other. But the good servant pleases his lord and does not worry about anything else but that his master be served and honored. Likewise, the true pastors and ministers of Jesus are persecuted, banished, and exiled,[70] because they don't care or worry about pleasing anyone but their Lord and master, serving, honoring, and valuing him. To him I pray not to send us others, but only those who ask for nothing else but his honor and glory and the edification of all. Amen.

Surely the end has come on my people, and they did not know that I *Amos 8* gave you some wheat [froment],[71] but I will change their feasts to lamenta- *Apoc. 18* tions, and all their songs to weeping. And her merchants will cry and shed tears on that great Babylon, saying, Woe, woe to her; she is fallen, the great *Jer. 51* Babylon, and has become a dwelling place of devils."[72] *Isa. 21*

Church. He turned once again to the Reformed Church, this time in Neuchâtel in 1539, but he and Calvin remained hostile to each other. In 1540, he made a final switch back to Catholicism. He disappeared after 1545.

70. Another reference to the banished Calvin and Farel.

71. The word *froment* (wheat) echoes the name of Dentière's husband, Antoine Froment, and acts as a veiled textual signature here at the end of the *Epistle*. The word recurs similarly near the end of Dentière's 1561 preface to Calvin's sermon. The imprint of Froment at the end of both works implies his involvement in those projects. Both works are framed by the wife's initials or name at the beginning and the husband's name at the end, suggesting that the couple collaborated on their production.

72. Babylon was a common name used by the reformers to designate the Roman Catholic Church, by analogy with the deportation and captivity of the Jews in Babylon, recounted in 2 Kings, when the Jews were denied religious freedom. The Book of Revelation, also known as the Apocalypse, compares Babylon to Rome; chapter 18 opens with an angel triumphantly proclaiming "Fallen, fallen is Babylon the great." The verse echoes Isaiah 21:9: "Fallen, fallen is Babylon, and all the images of her gods he has shattered in the ground."

SERMON OF M. JOHN CALVIN

on How Women Should Be Modest in Their Dress [1]

For all that is in the world, the lust of the flesh and the lust
of the eyes and the pride of life, is not of the Father but is of
the world. And the world passes away, and the lust of it;
but he who does the will of God abides forever.
—1 John 2:16–17 [2]

TO THE CHRISTIAN READER

Greetings in Jesus Christ our Lord
—M. D.

---

1. The title of the volume in which the preface appears is *The Behavior and Virtues Required of a Faithful Woman and Good Housekeeper: Contained in chapter XXI of the Proverbs of Solomon. Rendered in the form of a song by Théodore de Bèze. Plus a sermon on the modesty of Women in their Dress, by Monsieur John Calvin. In addition, several spiritual songs with music. M.D.LXI.* No place of publication is given. Rodolphe Peter and Jean-François Gilmont describe the two extant volumes containing the preface in *Bibliotheca Calviniana*, vol. 2, *Ecrits théologiques, littéraires et juridiques, 1555–1564;* they are entries 61/1 (Lunel, Bibliothèque municipale, Fonds Médard), 778–81; and 61/23 (Geneva, Musée Historique de la Réformation), 854–56. The Lunel volume is described in detail by J.-M. Hornus and R. Peter in "*Calviniana rarissima.*

2. The quotation from the First Epistle of John summarizes the particular lessons that Dentière's preface, Paul's verses, and Calvin's lesson all convey: All adornments of the body, whether rich or enticing clothing, makeup, or jewels, are, like the body itself, part of the temporal world. Rather than coveting or flaunting the things of the world, the Christian should concentrate on the eternal by following the will of God.

PREFACE TO A
SERMON BY JOHN CALVIN

Like those who guard a fortified place, reinforcing above all the spot that they know to be the weakest to prevent the enemy from getting in there, so we, seeing that there are in us several breaches through which Satan could enter, must mend and fortify the place in us that we know to be the hardest to guard, in order that he not get a foothold there. For because he is so experienced in that warfare, if he encroaches upon us the least little bit, I can tell you that that crafty, beguiling old felon will know how to take over the whole place. Therefore, just as we see that the enemy can often enter a city and sack it because its people have failed to repair a breach or to close the gates, in the same way, if we give Satan a place to enter, he will never stop until he has completely ruined and destroyed us. Now, since we must be on guard at the spot that is weakest in order to try harder to defend it, so also when we see that certain vices reign among us and that we are weak in that area, we must put our strength there so that Satan may not ransack and drag everything down to ruin.[3] That is how the prophets prevailed in combating and checking the spread of vice: Where vice and evil were the greatest, they applied the remedy so that evil would not gain any ground, and with extra force, prevailed over the enemy in the end and had him killed. That is what the pastors and ministers of God's word must do: Where they see that certain vices have caught on among the people in their care, they will endeavor to eradicate them by admonishing the people so that they will not spread any further—

3. The opening image of military vigilance elaborates on a more domestic version that Dentière had used in the *Epistle*: "And therefore I warn you to be on your guard, for if the father of the family knew that someone was supposed to rob his house by night, he would keep watch and would not let his house be ruined. And you, shouldn't you keep watch even more, seeing that the matter is greater, that it's a question of something much greater than a house, if not beyond all understanding?"

much as a surgeon applies the plaster or the hot iron where he knows the inflammation is greatest.

Now among the vices that reign today, makeup and excessive finery in clothing win the prize. As for makeup, Saint Cyprian makes it clear in a book he wrote about the apparel of virgins that the same vice existed in his time. He cannot hold back from saying that all makeup by which facial features are corrupted is the work of the devil. Ancient poets make fun of all herbs, oils, and other nonsense with which women make their faces ugly, believing they are making themselves more beautiful or keeping their complexions youthful (as they have used masks to do for a long time). Above all they deride ugly women, since it would be better that they be simply ugly than doubly so in painting their faces. For after the makeup has faded, the women seem more like a corpse, or a painted idol in a temple, long-covered with dust, than a live creature. In short, all makeup is nothing but a corruption of nature, or rather a combat against God, who does not will that his works be corrupted and counterfeited. I need only say—like that holy doctor and Saint Augustine after him—that using makeup erases the image of God in us, given that the image of God conveys something worth far more than the body's features. That is the first vice.

As for extravagant clothing, everything contrary to the use that God has ordained is bad. For seeing that continence and chastity are required of us, we should know that they do not consist only in our not giving free rein to the desires of our flesh, but also in sobriety and modesty of dress. And those men or women who are rich and have the means to own an infinite number of changes of clothes must not think that they have any greater license in this respect than others, since that would be to abuse rather than to use the wealth that God has given them in his liberality. "All things are lawful," says the Apostle, but not all things are helpful."[4] God wants us to use to our advantage the things he has given us to possess, but we must use them in good and helpful ways, and as he commanded. God gave man a voice, but we will not say that he should sing dirty and dissolute songs. God wanted iron to help us to plow the earth, not to be forged into swords and other weapons to help us kill each other. God gave us incense and myrrh and fire, but we should not offer sacrifice to idols. God gave us sheep in abundance, but it

1 Cor. 6

4. Dentière quotes Paul's First Epistle to the Corinthians, 6:12. In that passage, Paul warns the Corinthians against the behavior that had given their city a reputation for licentiousness. In the following verse, Paul writes, "The body is not meant for immorality, but for the Lord." In her preface to Calvin's sermon on Paul's Epistle to Timothy, Dentière follows a common practice in biblical commentary, that of glossing, or using another biblical quotation to help explain the quotation under commentary.

would be a terrible abuse to offer them in sacrifice to mute idols. The same is true for clothing, which, if we use, or rather abuse it in excess and too great abundance, we upset the ordinance of our God. And in fact, you will find that those who are the most concerned about adorning their bodies, are little concerned that their spirits be adorned with true, solid virtues. As for us, we should not seek the ornament of garments, but of good behavior.

As for women, who are in that regard more covetous than men, may they understand that too much daring has always been associated with immodesty; likewise, on the contrary, simplicity in clothes has always been a mark of chastity and continence. But so that we not go on too long about such an obvious thing, we would just have to request that the laws and edicts of the ancient emperors be kept and that the story of the mother of the Gracchi be known to all Christian women.[5] For it should make them ashamed to hear that a pagan woman had preferred to spend her wealth on the instruction of her children rather than on fancy and dissolute garments, like a woman from Campania in Italy, who competed with her about beautiful ornaments.[6] It is true that several women might resent this admonition, but I hope that, after having listened to the Apostle's exhortation, which is treated at length here, they will profit from it. For as the sage says, reprove a prudent man, and he will gain knowledge. And elsewhere, the ear that listens to correction in life, will lodge among the wise. As for the foolish women, we are not concerned with trying to please them. For even if you crush the fool in a mortar with a pestle among grains of wheat [*froment*][7] his folly will not depart from him. If anyone wants to learn more about that, let him read the treatise of Saint Cyprian that we have mentioned. Let us listen to the Apostle speak-

Suetonius,
Valerius
Maximus

Prov. 19:25

Prov. 15:31

Prov. 27:22

---

5. Roman sumptuary laws included the *Lex Oppia*, laws introduced in 215 B.C.E. to regulate conspicuous display by women; see Hunt, *Governance of the Consuming Passions*, 18–22. Cornelia was the daughter of Scipio Africanus and mother of two famous Roman tribunes, Tiberius and Gaius Gracchus. After her husband's death she devoted herself to careful management of her household and to her children's education. Ancient historians, including Suetonius and Valerius Maximus, admired her discretion and noble ideals and praised her devotion as a mother. In *The Education of a Christian Woman*, Vives mentions the *Lex Oppia* and refers frequently to Cornelia.

6. In book 2, chapter 10 of *The Education of a Christian Woman*, Vives recounts this story taken from Valerius Maximus: "A certain wealthy woman from Campania came to Rome and was welcomed into the home of Cornelia, the wife of Gracchus, and she spread out all her feminine adornments, for she was rich in precious metals, wardrobe, and jewelry. When Cornelia had congratulated her on her splendor, the Campanian woman asked if Cornelia would mind showing her her precious jewels. The two young Gracchi had gone off to school. She answered that she would do so in the evening. When the children returned, she said, 'These are my only treasures'" (269).

7. As she does toward the end of the *Very Useful Epistle*, Dentière slips in a reference to wheat [*froment*], thereby inserting her husband Antoine Froment's name at the end of her preface.

ing to Timothy and to the man who preached publicly about that passage, a man who because of the purity of his teachings deserves to be heard among all the ministers and faithful pastors in Europe today. Therefore if we are assaulted by some bad, excessive affection as we have said, let us repair the breach immediately and prevent the devil from surprising us, entering within us, and toppling us to ruin. May the Lord give grace to all of us. Amen.

SERIES EDITORS'
BIBLIOGRAPHY

Note: Items listed in the volume editor's bibliography are not repeated here.

PRIMARY SOURCES

Alberti, Leon Battista (1404–72). *The Family in Renaissance Florence.* Trans. Renée Neu Watkins. Columbia, SC: University of South Carolina Press, 1969.

Arenal, Electa, and Stacey Schlau, eds. *Untold Sisters: Hispanic Nuns in Their Own Works.* Trans. Amanda Powell. Albuquerque, NM: University of New Mexico Press, 1989.

Astell, Mary (1666–1731). *The First English Feminist: Reflections on Marriage and Other Writings.* Ed. Bridget Hill. New York: St. Martin's Press, 1986.

Atherton, Margaret, ed. *Women Philosophers of the Early Modern Period.* Indianapolis, IN: Hackett, 1994.

Aughterson, Kate, ed. *Renaissance Woman: Constructions of Femininity in England: A Source Book.* London and New York: Routledge, 1995.

Barbaro, Francesco (1390–1454). *On Wifely Duties.* Trans. Benjamin Kohl. In *The Earthly Republic,* ed. Benjamin Kohl and R. G. Witt, 179–228. Philadelphia: University of Pennsylvania Press, 1978. Translation of the preface and Book 2.

Behn, Aphra. *The Works of Aphra Behn.* 7 vols. Ed. Janet Todd. Columbus: Ohio State University Press, 1992–96.

Boccaccio, Giovanni (1313–75). *Famous Women.* Ed. and trans. Virginia Brown. The I Tatti Renaissance Library. Cambridge, MA: Harvard University Press, 2001.

———. *Corbaccio or the Labyrinth of Love.* Trans. Anthony K. Cassell. 2d rev. ed. Binghamton, NY: Medieval and Renaissance Texts and Studies, 1993.

Bruni, Leonardo (1370–1444). "On the Study of Literature (1405) to Lady Battista Malatesta of Montefeltro." In *The Humanism of Leonardo Bruni: Selected Texts,* trans. Gordon Griffiths, James Hankins, and David Thompson, 240–51. Binghamton, NY: Medieval and Renaissance Texts and Studies, 1987.

Castiglione, Baldassare (1478–1529). *The Book of the Courtier.* Trans. George Bull. New York: Penguin, 1967.

Cerasano, S. P., and Marion Wynne-Davies, eds. *Readings in Renaissance Women's Drama:*

Criticism, History, and Performance, 1594–1998. London and New York: Routledge, 1998.

Christine de Pizan (1365–1431). *The Book of the City of Ladies.* Trans. Earl Jeffrey Richards. Foreword by Marina Warner. New York: Persea Books, 1982.

———. *The Treasure of the City of Ladies.* Trans. Sarah Lawson. New York: Viking Penguin, 1985.

———. *The Treasure of the City of Ladies.* Trans. Charity Cannon Willard. Ed. Madeleine P. Cosman. New York: Persea Books, 1989.

Clarke, Danielle, ed. *Isabella Whitney, Mary Sidney, and Aemilia Lanyer: Renaissance Women Poets.* New York: Penguin Books, 2000.

Crawford, Patricia, and Laura Gowing, eds. *Women's Worlds in Seventeenth-Century England: A Source Book.* London and New York: Routledge, 2000.

Daybell, James, ed. *Early Modern Women's Letter Writing, 1450–1700.* Houndmills, England, and New York: Palgrave, 2001.

Elizabeth I: Collected Works. Ed. Leah S. Marcus, Janel Mueller, and Mary Beth Rose. Chicago: University of Chicago Press, 2000.

Elyot, Thomas (1490–1546). *Defence of Good Women: The Feminist Controversy of the Renaissance.* Facsimile Reproductions. Ed. Diane Bornstein. New York: Delmar, 1980.

Erasmus, Desiderius (1467–1536). *Erasmus on Women.* Ed. Erika Rummel. Toronto: University of Toronto Press, 1996.

Female and Male Voices in Early Modern England: An Anthology of Renaissance Writing. Ed. Betty S. Travitsky and Anne Lake Prescott. New York: Columbia University Press, 2000.

Ferguson, Moira, ed. *First Feminists: British Women Writers 1578–1799.* Bloomington: Indiana University Press, 1985.

Galilei, Maria Celeste. *Sister Maria Celeste's Letters to Her Father, Galileo.* Ed. and trans. Rinaldina Russell. Lincoln, NE, and New York: Writers Club Press of Universe.com, 2000.

Gethner, Perry, ed. *The Lunatic Lover and Other Plays by French Women of the Seventeenth and Eighteenth Centuries.* Portsmouth, NH: Heinemann, 1994.

Glückel of Hameln (1646–1724). *The Memoirs of Glückel of Hameln.* Trans. Marvin Lowenthal. New intro. by Robert Rosen. New York: Schocken Books, 1977.

Henderson, Katherine Usher, and Barbara F. McManus, eds. *Half Humankind: Contexts and Texts of the Controversy about Women in England, 1540–1640.* Bloomington: Indiana University Press, 1985.

Humanist Educational Treatises. Ed. and trans. Craig W. Kallendorf. The I Tatti Renaissance Library. Cambridge, MA: Harvard University Press, 2002.

Joscelin, Elizabeth. *The Mothers Legacy to Her Unborn Childe.* Ed. Jean leDrew Metcalfe. Toronto: University of Toronto Press, 2000.

Kaminsky, Amy Katz, ed. *Water Lilies, Flores del Agua: An Anthology of Spanish Women Writers from the Fifteenth through the Nineteenth Century.* Minneapolis: University of Minnesota Press, 1996.

Kempe, Margery (1373–1439). *The Book of Margery Kempe.* Trans. and ed. Lynn Staley. Norton Critical Editions. New York: W. W. Norton, 2001.

King, Margaret L., and Albert Rabil Jr., eds. *Her Immaculate Hand: Selected Works by and about the Women Humanists of Quattrocento Italy.* 2d rev. paperback ed. 1983. Reprint, Binghamton, NY: Medieval and Renaissance Texts and Studies, 1991.

Klein, Joan Larsen, ed. *Daughters, Wives, and Widows: Writings by Men about Women and Marriage in England, 1500–1640.* Urbana: University of Illinois Press, 1992.

Knox, John (1505–72). *The Political Writings of John Knox: The First Blast of the Trumpet against the Monstrous Regiment of Women and Other Selected Works.* Ed. Marvin A. Breslow. Washington: Folger Shakespeare Library, 1985.

Kors, Alan C., and Edward Peters, eds. *Witchcraft in Europe, 400–1700: A Documentary History.* Philadelphia: University of Pennsylvania Press, 2000.

Krämer, Heinrich, and Jacob Sprenger. *Malleus Maleficarum* (ca. 1487). Trans. Montague Summers. London: Pushkin Press, 1928; reprint, New York: Dover, 1971.

Larsen, Anne R., and Colette H. Winn, eds. *Writings by Pre-Revolutionary French Women: From Marie de France to Elizabeth Vigée-Le Brun.* New York and London: Garland, 2000.

Lorris, William de, and Jean de Meun. *The Romance of the Rose.* Trans. Charles Dahlbert. Princeton, NJ: Princeton University Press, 1971; reprint, University Press of New England, 1983.

Mary of Agreda. *The Divine Life of the Most Holy Virgin.* Abridgment of *The Mystical City of God.* Abr. by Fr. Bonaventure Amedeo de Caesarea, M.C. Trans. from French by Abbé Joseph A. Boullan. Rockford, IL: Tan Books, 1997.

Myers, Kathleen A., and Amanda Powell, eds. *A Wild Country Out in the Garden: The Spiritual Journals of a Colonial Mexican Nun.* Bloomington: Indiana University Press, 1999.

Russell, Rinaldina, ed. *Sister Maria Celeste's Letters to Her Father, Galileo.* San Jose, CA, and New York: Writers Club Press, 2000.

Teresa of Avila, Saint (1515–82). *The Life of Saint Teresa of Avila by Herself.* Trans. J. M. Cohen. New York: Viking Penguin, 1957.

Weyer, Johann (1515–88). *Witches, Devils, and Doctors in the Renaissance: Johann Weyer, De praestigiis daemonum.* Ed. George Mora with Benjamin G. Kohl, Erik Midelfort, and Helen Bacon. Trans. John Shea. Binghamton, NY: Medieval and Renaissance Texts and Studies, 1991.

Wilson, Katharina M., ed. *Medieval Women Writers.* Athens: University of Georgia Press, 1984.

———, ed. *Women Writers of the Renaissance and Reformation.* Athens: University of Georgia Press, 1987.

———, and Frank J. Warnke, eds. *Women Writers of the Seventeenth Century.* Athens: University of Georgia Press, 1989.

Wollstonecraft, Mary. *A Vindication of the Rights of Men and a Vindication of the Rights of Women.* Ed. Sylvana Tomaselli. Cambridge: Cambridge University Press, 1995.

———. *The Vindications of the Rights of Men, the Rights of Women.* Ed. D. L. Macdonald and Kathleen Scherf. Peterborough, Ontario, Canada: Broadview Press, 1997.

Women Critics 1660–1820: An Anthology. Edited by the Folger Collective on Early Women Critics. Bloomington: Indiana University Press, 1995.

Women Writers in English, 1350–1850. Fifteen volumes published through 1999 (projected thirty-volume series suspended). New York and Oxford: Oxford University Press.

Wroth, Lady Mary. *The Countess of Montgomery's Urania.* 2 parts. Ed. Josephine A. Roberts. Tempe, AZ: Medieval and Renaissance Texts and Studies, 1995, 1999.

———. *Lady Mary Wroth's "Love's Victory": The Penshurst Manuscript.* Ed. Michael G. Brennan. London: The Roxburghe Club, 1988.

————. *The Poems of Lady Mary Wroth.* Ed. Josephine A. Roberts. Baton Rouge: Louisiana State University Press, 1983.

Zayas, Maria de. *The Disenchantments of Love.* Trans. H. Patsy Boyer. Albany: State University of New York Press, 1997.

————. *The Enchantments of Love: Amorous and Exemplary Novels.* Trans. H. Patsy Boyer. Berkeley and Los Angeles: University of California Press, 1990.

SECONDARY SOURCES

Ahlgren, Gillian. *Teresa of Avila and the Politics of Sanctity.* Ithaca, NY: Cornell University Press, 1996.

Akkerman, Tjitske, and Siep Sturman, eds. *Feminist Thought in European History, 1400–2000.* London and New York: Routledge, 1997.

Backer, Anne Liot. *Precious Women.* New York: Basic Books, 1974.

Barash, Carol. *English Women's Poetry, 1649–1714: Politics, Community, and Linguistic Authority.* New York and Oxford: Oxford University Press, 1996.

Battigelli, Anna. *Margaret Cavendish and the Exiles of the Mind.* Lexington: University of Kentucky Press, 1998.

Beasley, Faith. *Revising Memory: Women's Fiction and Memoirs in Seventeenth-Century France.* New Brunswick: Rutgers University Press, 1990.

Beilin, Elaine V. *Redeeming Eve: Women Writers of the English Renaissance.* Princeton, NJ: Princeton University Press, 1987.

Benson, Pamela Joseph. *The Invention of Renaissance Woman: The Challenge of Female Independence in the Literature and Thought of Italy and England.* University Park: Pennsylvania State University Press, 1992.

Bilinkoff, Jodi. *The Avila of Saint Teresa: Religious Reform in a Sixteenth-Century City.* Ithaca, NY: Cornell University Press, 1989.

Bissell, R. Ward. *Artemisia Gentileschi and the Authority of Art.* University Park: Pennsylvania State University Press, 2000.

Blain, Virginia, Isobel Grundy, and Patricia Clements, eds. *The Feminist Companion to Literature in English: Women Writers from the Middle Ages to the Present.* New Haven, CT: Yale University Press, 1990.

Bornstein, Daniel, and Roberto Rusconi, eds. *Women and Religion in Medieval and Renaissance Italy.* Trans. Margery J. Schneider. Chicago: University of Chicago Press, 1996.

Brant, Clare, and Diane Purkiss, eds. *Women, Texts and Histories, 1575–1760.* London and New York: Routledge, 1992.

Briggs, Robin. *Witches and Neighbours: The Social and Cultural Context of European Witchcraft.* New York: HarperCollins, 1995; Viking Penguin, 1996.

Brink, Jean R., ed. *Female Scholars: A Tradition of Learned Women before 1800.* Montréal: Eden Press Women's Publications, 1980.

Brown, Judith C. *Immodest Acts: The Life of a Lesbian Nun in Renaissance Italy.* New York: Oxford University Press, 1986.

Bynum, Carolyn Walker. *Holy Feast and Holy Fast: The Religious Significance of Food to Medieval Women.* Berkeley and Los Angeles: University of California Press, 1987.

Cervigni, Dino S., ed. *Women Mystic Writers. Annali d'Italianistica* 13 (1995): entire issue.

————, and Rebecca West, eds. *Women's Voices in Italian Literature. Annali d'Italianistica* 7 (1989): entire issue.

Charlton, Kenneth. *Women, Religion and Education in Early Modern England.* London and New York: Routledge, 1999.

Chojnacka, Monica. *Working Women in Early Modern Venice.* Baltimore, MD: Johns Hopkins University Press, 2001.

Chojnacki, Stanley. *Women and Men in Renaissance Venice: Twelve Essays on Patrician Society.* Baltimore, MD: Johns Hopkins University Press, 2000.

Cholakian, Patricia Francis. *Rape and Writing in the* Heptameron *of Marguerite de Navarre.* Carbondale and Edwardsville: Southern Illinois University Press, 1991.

————. *Women and the Politics of Self-Representation in Seventeenth-Century France.* Newark: University of Delaware Press, 2000.

Clogan, Paul Maruice, ed. *Medievali et Humanistica: Literacy and the Lay Reader.* Lanham, MD: Rowman & Littlefield, 2000.

Conley, John J., S.J. *The Suspicion of Virtue: Women Philosophers in Neoclassical France.* Ithaca, NY: Cornell University Press, 2002.

Crabb, Ann. *The Strozzi of Florence: Widowhood and Family Solidarity in the Renaissance.* Ann Arbor: University of Michigan Press, 2000.

Cruz, Anne J., and Mary Elizabeth Perry, eds. *Culture and Control in Counter-Reformation Spain.* Minneapolis: University of Minnesota Press, 1992.

Davis, Natalie Zemon. *Women on the Margins: Three Seventeenth-Century Lives.* Cambridge, MA: Harvard University Press, 1995.

DeJean, Joan. *Ancients against Moderns: Culture Wars and the Making of a Fin de Siècle.* Chicago: University of Chicago Press, 1997.

————. *Tender Geographies: Women and the Origins of the Novel in France.* New York: Columbia University Press, 1991.

Dixon, Laurinda S. *Perilous Chastity: Women and Illness in Pre-Enlightenment Art and Medicine.* Ithaca, NY: Cornell University Press, 1995.

Dolan, Frances, E. *Whores of Babylon: Catholicism, Gender, and Seventeenth-Century Print Culture.* Ithaca, NY: Cornell University Press, 1999.

Donovan, Josephine. *Women and the Rise of the Novel, 1405–1726.* New York: St. Martin's Press, 1999.

Erauso, Catalina de. *Lieutenant Nun: Memoir of a Basque Transvestite in the New World.* Trans. Michele Stepto and Gabriel Stepto, with a foreword by Marjorie Garber. Boston: Beacon Press, 1995.

Erickson, Amy Louise. *Women and Property in Early Modern England.* London and New York: Routledge, 1993.

Ezell, Margaret J. M. *The Patriarch's Wife: Literary Evidence and the History of the Family.* Chapel Hill: University of North Carolina Press, 1987.

————. *Social Authorship and the Advent of Print.* Baltimore, MD: Johns Hopkins University Press, 1999.

————. *Writing Women's Literary History.* Baltimore, MD: Johns Hopkins University Press, 1993.

Fletcher, Anthony. *Gender, Sex, and Subordination in England, 1500–1800.* New Haven, CT: Yale University Press, 1995.

Frye, Susan, and Karen Robertson, eds. *Maids and Mistresses, Cousins and Queens: Women's Alliances in Early Modern England.* Oxford: Oxford University Press, 1999.

Gallagher, Catherine. *Nobody's Story: The Vanishing Acts of Women Writers in the Marketplace, 1670–1820.* Berkeley and Los Angeles: University of California Press, 1994.

Garrard, Mary D. *Artemisia Gentileschi: The Image of the Female Hero in Italian Baroque Art.* Princeton, NJ: Princeton University Press, 1989.

Gelbart, Nina Rattner. *The King's Midwife: A History and Mystery of Madame du Coudray.* Berkeley and Los Angeles: University of California Press, 1998.

Goldberg, Jonathan. *Desiring Women Writing: English Renaissance Examples.* Stanford, CA: Stanford University Press, 1997.

Goldsmith, Elizabeth C. *Exclusive Conversations: The Art of Interaction in Seventeenth-Century France.* Philadelphia: University of Pennsylvania Press, 1988.

———, ed. *Writing the Female Voice.* Boston: Northeastern University Press, 1989.

———, and Dena Goodman, eds. *Going Public: Women and Publishing in Early Modern France.* Ithaca, NY: Cornell University Press, 1995.

Greer, Margaret Rich. *Maria de Zayas Tells Baroque Tales of Love and the Cruelty of Men.* University Park: Pennsylvania State University Press, 2000.

Hackett, Helen. *Women and Romance Fiction in the English Renaissance.* Cambridge: Cambridge University Press, 2000.

Hall, Kim F. *Things of Darkness: Economies of Race and Gender in Early Modern England.* Ithaca, NY: Cornell University Press, 1995.

Hampton, Timothy. *Literature and the Nation in the Sixteenth Century: Inventing Renaissance France.* Ithaca, NY: Cornell University Press, 2001.

Hardwick, Julie. *The Practice of Patriarchy: Gender and the Politics of Household Authority in Early Modern France.* University Park: Pennsylvania State University Press, 1998.

Harth, Erica. *Ideology and Culture in Seventeenth-Century France.* Ithaca, NY: Cornell University Press, 1983.

———. *Cartesian Women. Versions and Subversions of Rational Discourse in the Old Regime.* Ithaca, NY: Cornell University Press, 1992.

Haselkorn, Anne M., and Betty Travitsky, eds. *The Renaissance Englishwoman in Print: Counterbalancing the Canon.* Amherst: University of Massachusetts Press, 1990.

Herlihy, David. "Did Women Have a Renaissance? A Reconsideration." *Medievalia et Humanistica* n.s., 13 (1985): 1–22.

Hill, Bridget. *The Republican Virago: The Life and Times of Catharine Macaulay, Historian.* New York: Oxford University Press, 1992.

A History of Women in the West. Vol. 1. *From Ancient Goddesses to Christian Saints.* Ed. Pauline Schmitt Pantel. Vol. 2. *Silences of the Middle Ages.* Ed. Christiane Klapisch-Zuber. Vol. 3. *Renaissance and Enlightenment Paradoxes.* Ed. Natalie Zemon Davis and Arlette Farge. Cambridge, MA: Harvard University Press, 1992–93.

Hobby, Elaine. *Virtue of Necessity: English Women's Writing, 1646–1688.* London: Virago Press, 1988.

Horowitz, Maryanne Cline. "Aristotle and Women." *Journal of the History of Biology* 9 (1976): 183–213.

Hufton, Olwen H. *The Prospect before Her: A History of Women in Western Europe.* Vol. 1. *1500–1800.* New York: HarperCollins, 1996.

Hull, Suzanne W. *Chaste, Silent, and Obedient: English Books for Women, 1475–1640.* San Marino, CA: Huntington Library, 1982.

Hunt, Lynn, ed. *The Invention of Pornography: Obscenity and the Origins of Modernity, 1500–1800.* New York: Zone Books, 1996.

Hutner, Heidi, ed. *Rereading Aphra Behn: History, Theory, and Criticism.* Charlottesville: University Press of Virginia, 1993.

Hutson, Lorna, ed. *Feminism and Renaissance Studies.* New York: Oxford University Press, 1999.

James, Susan E. *Kateryn Parr: The Making of a Queen.* Aldershot and Brookfield: Ashgate, 1999.

Jankowski, Theodora A. *Women in Power in the Early Modern Drama.* Urbana: University of Illinois Press, 1992.

Jansen, Katherine Ludwig. *The Making of the Magdalen: Preaching and Popular Devotion in the Later Middle Ages.* Princeton, NJ: Princeton University Press, 2000.

Jed, Stephanie H. *Chaste Thinking: The Rape of Lucretia and the Birth of Humanism.* Bloomington: Indiana University Press, 1989.

Kagan, Richard L. *Lucrecia's Dreams: Politics and Prophecy in Sixteenth-Century Spain.* Berkeley and Los Angeles: University of California Press, 1990.

Kelly, Joan. "Did Women Have a Renaissance?" In *Women, History, and Theory.* Chicago: University of Chicago Press, 1984. Reprinted in *Becoming Visible: Women in European History,* ed. Renate Bridenthal, Claudia Koonz, and Susan M. Stuard. 3d ed. Boston: Houghton Mifflin, 1998.

―――. "Early Feminist Theory and the *Querelle des Femmes.*" In *Women, History, and Theory.*

Kelso, Ruth. *Doctrine for the Lady of the Renaissance.* Foreword by Katharine M. Rogers. Urbana: University of Illinois Press, 1956, 1978.

King, Carole. *Renaissance Women Patrons: Wives and Widows in Italy, c. 1300–1550.* New York and Manchester: Manchester University Press (distributed in the United States by St. Martin's Press), 1998.

King, Margaret L. *Women of the Renaissance.* Foreword by Catharine R. Stimpson. Chicago: University of Chicago Press, 1991.

Krontiris, Tina. *Oppositional Voices: Women as Writers and Translators of Literature in the English Renaissance.* London and New York: Routledge, 1992.

Kuehn, Thomas. *Law, Family, and Women: Toward a Legal Anthropology of Renaissance Italy.* Chicago: University of Chicago Press, 1991.

Kunze, Bonnelyn Young. *Margaret Fell and the Rise of Quakerism.* Stanford, CA: Stanford University Press, 1994.

Labalme, Patricia A., ed. *Beyond Their Sex: Learned Women of the European Past.* New York: New York University Press, 1980.

Laqueur, Thomas. *Making Sex: Body and Gender from the Greeks to Freud.* Cambridge, MA: Harvard University Press, 1990.

Larsen, Anne R., and Colette H. Winn, eds. *Renaissance Women Writers: French Texts/ American Contexts.* Detroit, MI: Wayne State University Press, 1994.

Lerner, Gerda. *The Creation of Patriarchy* and *Creation of Feminist Consciousness, 1000–1870.* 2 vols. New York: Oxford University Press, 1986, 1994.

Levin, Carole, and Jeanie Watson, eds. *Ambiguous Realities: Women in the Middle Ages and Renaissance.* Detroit, MI: Wayne State University Press, 1987.

―――, et al. *Extraordinary Women of the Medieval and Renaissance World: A Biographical Dictionary.* Westport, CT: Greenwood Press, 2000.

Lindsey, Karen. *Divorced, Beheaded, Survived: A Feminist Reinterpretation of the Wives of Henry VIII.* Reading, MA: Addison-Wesley, 1995.

Lochrie, Karma. *Margery Kempe and Translations of the Flesh*. Philadelphia: University of Pennsylvania Press, 1992.

Lougee, Carolyn C. *Le Paradis des Femmes: Women, Salons, and Social Stratification in Seventeenth-Century France*. Princeton, NJ: Princeton University Press, 1976.

Love, Harold. *The Culture and Commerce of Texts: Scribal Publication in Seventeenth-Century England*. Amherst: University of Massachusetts Press, 1993.

MacCarthy, Bridget G. *The Female Pen: Women Writers and Novelists 1621–1818*. Preface by Janet Todd. 1946–47. Reprint, New York: New York University Press, 1994.

Maclean, Ian. *Woman Triumphant: Feminism in French Literature, 1610–1652*. Oxford: Clarendon Press, 1977.

Matter, E. Ann, and John Coakley, eds. *Creative Women in Medieval and Early Modern Italy*. Philadelphia: University of Pennsylvania Press, 1994 (sequel to the Monson collection, below).

McLeod, Glenda. *Virtue and Venom: Catalogs of Women from Antiquity to the Renaissance*. Ann Arbor: University of Michigan Press, 1991.

Meek, Christine, ed. *Women in Renaissance and Early Modern Europe*. Dublin-Portland: Four Courts Press, 2000.

Mendelson, Sara, and Patricia Crawford. *Women in Early Modern England, 1550–1720*. Oxford: Clarendon Press, 1998.

Merrim, Stephanie. *Early Modern Women's Writing and Sor Juana Inés de la Cruz*. Nashville, TN: Vanderbilt University Press, 1999.

Messbarger, Rebecca. *The Century of Women: The Representations of Women in Eighteenth-Century Italian Public Discourse*. Toronto: University of Toronto Press, 2002.

Miller, Nancy K. *The Heroine's Text: Readings in the French and English Novel, 1722–1782*. New York: Columbia University Press, 1980.

Miller, Naomi J. *Changing the Subject: Mary Wroth and Figurations of Gender in Early Modern England*. Lexington, KY: University Press of Kentucky, 1996.

————, and Gary Waller, eds. *Reading Mary Wroth: Representing Alternatives in Early Modern England*. Knoxville, TN: University of Tennessee Press, 1991.

Monson, Craig A., ed. *The Crannied Wall: Women, Religion, and the Arts in Early Modern Europe*. Ann Arbor: University of Michigan Press, 1992.

Newman, Karen. *Fashioning Femininity and English Renaissance Drama*. Chicago and London: University of Chicago Press, 1991.

Okin, Susan Moller. *Women in Western Political Thought*. Princeton, NJ: Princeton University Press, 1979.

Ozment, Steven. *The Bürgermeister's Daughter: Scandal in a Sixteenth-Century German Town*. New York: St. Martin's Press, 1995.

Pacheco, Anita, ed. *Early [English] Women Writers: 1600–1720*. New York and London: Longman, 1998.

Pagels, Elaine. *Adam, Eve, and the Serpent*. New York: Harper Collins, 1988.

Panizza, Letizia, ed. *Women in Italian Renaissance Culture and Society*. Oxford: European Humanities Research Centre, 2000.

————, and Sharon Wood, eds. *A History of Women's Writing in Italy*. Cambridge: Cambridge University Press, 2000.

Perry, Mary Elizabeth. *Crime and Society in Early Modern Seville*. Hanover, NH: University Press of New England, 1980.

————. *Gender and Disorder in Early Modern Seville*. Princeton, NJ: Princeton University Press, 1990.

Petroff, Elizabeth Alvilda, ed. *Medieval Women's Visionary Literature.* New York: Oxford University Press, 1986.

Perry, Ruth. *The Celebrated Mary Astell: An Early English Feminist.* Chicago: University of Chicago Press, 1986.

Rabil, Albert. *Laura Cereta: Quattrocento Humanist.* Binghamton, NY: Medieval and Renaissance Texts and Studies, 1981.

Rapley, Elizabeth. *A Social History of the Cloister: Daily Life in the Teaching Monasteries of the Old Regime.* Montreal: McGill-Queen's University Press, 2001.

Raven, James, Helen Small, and Naomi Tadmor, eds. *The Practice and Representation of Reading in England.* Cambridge: University Press, 1996.

Reardon, Colleen. *Holy Concord within Sacred Walls: Nuns and Music in Siena, 1575–1700.* Oxford: Oxford University Press, 2001.

Reiss, Sheryl E., and David G. Wilkins, ed. *Beyond Isabella: Secular Women Patrons of Art in Renaissance Italy.* Kirksville, MO: Truman State University Press, 2001.

Rheubottom, David. *Age, Marriage, and Politics in Fifteenth-Century Ragusa.* Oxford: Oxford University Press, 2000.

Richardson, Brian. *Printing, Writers, and Readers in Renaissance Italy.* Cambridge: University Press, 1999.

Riddle, John M. *Contraception and Abortion from the Ancient World to the Renaissance.* Cambridge, MA: Harvard University Press, 1992.

———. *Eve's Herbs: A History of Contraception and Abortion in the West.* Cambridge, MA: Harvard University Press, 1997.

Rose, Mary Beth. *The Expense of Spirit: Love and Sexuality in English Renaissance Drama.* Ithaca, NY: Cornell University Press, 1988.

———. *Gender and Heroism in Early Modern English Literature.* Chicago: University of Chicago Press, 2002.

———, ed. *Women in the Middle Ages and the Renaissance: Literary and Historical Perspectives.* Syracuse: Syracuse University Press, 1986.

Rosenthal, Margaret F. *The Honest Courtesan: Veronica Franco, Citizen and Writer in Sixteenth-Century Venice.* Foreword by Catharine R. Stimpson. Chicago: University of Chicago Press, 1992.

Sackville-West, Vita. *Daughter of France: The Life of La Grande Mademoiselle.* Garden City, NY: Doubleday, 1959.

Schiebinger, Londa. *The Mind Has No Sex? Women in the Origins of Modern Science.* Cambridge, MA: Harvard University Press, 1991.

———. *Nature's Body: Gender in the Making of Modern Science.* Boston: Beacon Press, 1993.

Schutte, Anne Jacobson, Thomas Kuehn, and Silvana Seidel Menchi, eds. *Time, Space, and Women's Lives in Early Modern Europe.* Kirksville, MO: Truman State University Press, 2001.

Shannon, Laurie. *Sovereign Amity: Figures of Friendship in Shakespearean Contexts.* Chicago: University of Chicago Press, 2002.

Shemek, Deanna. *Ladies Errant: Wayward Women and Social Order in Early Modern Italy.* Durham, NC: Duke University Press, 1998.

Sobel, Dava. *Galileo's Daughter: A Historical Memoir of Science, Faith, and Love.* New York: Penguin Books, 2000.

Sommerville, Margaret R. *Sex and Subjection: Attitudes to Women in Early-Modern Society.* London: Arnold, 1995.

Spencer, Jane. *The Rise of the Woman Novelist: From Aphra Behn to Jane Austen.* Oxford: Basil Blackwell, 1986.

Spender, Dale. *Mothers of the Novel: One Hundred Good Women Writers before Jane Austen.* London and New York: Routledge, 1986.

Sperling, Jutta Gisela. *Convents and the Body Politic in Late Renaissance Venice.* Foreword by Catharine R. Stimpson. Chicago: University of Chicago Press, 1999.

Steinbrügge, Lieselotte. *The Moral Sex: Woman's Nature in the French Enlightenment.* Trans. Pamela E. Selwyn. New York: Oxford University Press, 1995.

Stephens, Sonya, ed. *A History of Women's Writing in France.* Cambridge: Cambridge University Press, 2000.

Stuard, Susan M. "The Dominion of Gender: Women's Fortunes in the High Middle Ages." In *Becoming Visible: Women in European History,* ed. Renate Bridenthal, Claudia Koonz, and Susan M. Stuard. 3d ed. Boston: Houghton Mifflin, 1998.

Summit, Jennifer. *Lost Property: The Woman Writer and English Literary History, 1380–1589.* Chicago: University of Chicago Press, 2000.

Surtz, Ronald E. *The Guitar of God: Gender, Power, and Authority in the Visionary World of Mother Juana de la Cruz (1481–1534).* Philadelphia: University of Pennsylvania Press, 1991.

———. *Writing Women in Late Medieval and Early Modern Spain.* Philadelphia: University of Pennsylvania Press, 1995.

Teague, Frances. *Bathsua Makin, Woman of Learning.* Lewisburg, PA: Bucknell University Press, 1999.

Todd, Janet. *The Secret Life of Aphra Behn.* London, New York, and Sydney: Pandora, 2000.

———. *The Sign of Angelica: Women, Writing, and Fiction, 1660–1800.* New York: Columbia University Press, 1989.

Van Dijk, Susan; Lia van Gemert; and Sheila Ottway, eds. *Writing the History of Women's Writing: Toward an International Approach.* Proceedings of the Colloquium, Amsterdam, 9–11 September. Amsterdam: Royal Netherlands Academy of Arts and Sciences, 2001.

Waithe, Mary Ellen, ed. *A History of Women Philosophers.* 3 vols. Dordrecht, Holland: Martinus Nijhoff, 1987.

Wall, Wendy. *The Imprint of Gender: Authorship and Publication in the English Renaissance.* Ithaca, NY: Cornell University Press, 1993.

Walsh, William T. *St. Teresa of Avila: A Biography.* Rockford, IL: TAN Books, 1987.

Warnicke, Retha M. *The Marrying of Anne of Cleves: Royal Protocol in Tudor England.* Cambridge: Cambridge University Press, 2000.

Watt, Diane. *Secretaries of God: Women Prophets in Late Medieval and Early Modern England.* Cambridge: D. S. Brewer, 1997.

Weber, Alison. *Teresa of Avila and the Rhetoric of Femininity.* Princeton, NJ: Princeton University Press, 1990.

Welles, Marcia L. *Persephone's Girdle: Narratives of Rape in Seventeenth-Century Spanish Literature.* Nashville, TN: Vanderbilt University Press, 2000.

Whitehead, Barbara J., ed. *Women's Education in Early Modern Europe: A History, 1500–1800.* New York and London: Garland, 1999.

Wiesner, Merry E. *Women and Gender in Early Modern Europe.* Cambridge: Cambridge University Press, 1993.

————. *Working Women in Renaissance Germany.* New Brunswick, NJ: Rutgers University Press, 1986.

Willard, Charity Cannon. *Christine de Pizan: Her Life and Works.* New York: Persea Books, 1984.

Wilson, Katharina, ed. *An Encyclopedia of Continental Women Writers.* New York: Garland, 1991.

Woodbridge, Linda. *Women and the English Renaissance: Literature and the Nature of Womankind, 1540–1620.* Urbana: University of Illinois Press, 1984.

Woods, Susanne. *Lanyer: A Renaissance Woman Poet.* New York: Oxford University Press, 1999.

————, and Margaret P. Hannay, eds. *Teaching Tudor and Stuart Women Writers.* New York: MLA, 2000.

INDEX